DEFY YOUR GRAVITY

NEHA GOEL / DRISHTI GOEL

Rise Above Your Challenges & Embrace Your Potential

ISBN 979-8-89610-700-2

Cover Design & Illustrations by : Prakash Narkhede

Book Layout by : Anshika Digital Media, Delhi

This book is lovingly dedicated to my beloved father, *Late Shri V.P. Modi*—a devoted husband, father, cherished grandfather, and prolific writer. Your wisdom, values, and unwavering support continue to guide us, and your legacy inspires every word inscribed within these pages.

Neha

Defy means to challenge or resist something, while ***gravity***, in this context, refers to the limitations that hold us back: fear, self-doubt, or negative thoughts. Thus, ***Defy Your Gravity*** is about rising above our challenges and embracing our potential. The moment we make the choice, we can break free from everything that weighs us down and strive for a more fulfilling life.

A PERSONAL MESSAGE FOR YOU
Take It Slow, and Let It Grow

Our intention to write every word, every story, and every reflection exercise here is to empower you to know yourself better. And once you do that, it'll be easier for you to ***defy your gravity.***

Read slowly, absorb each thought, reflect, and practice the exercises mentioned at the end of each chapter to derive deeper insights that will empower your individual transformational journey.

Reading the last few chapters might seem a bit overwhelming, but we urge you to please take your time, read at your own pace, pause when you have to, and finish reading the whole book.

We have always found the practice of learning and maintaining a list of all the new words from a book very helpful, so grab a highlighter and a pencil as you explore new vocabulary along the way!

Read this book with an open mind. One word at a time, one chapter at a time – you'll get there.

Let's begin.

CONTENTS

PREFACE

"Stories you read when you're the right age never quite leave you. You may forget who wrote them or what the story was called. Sometimes you'll forget precisely what happened, but if a story touches you, it will stay with you, haunting the places in your mind that you rarely ever visit."

– Neil Gaiman, M Is for Magic

Stories can indeed be very impactful. They have a unique power to touch our hearts through their emotions and lessons that stay with us throughout our lives. Through *Defy Your Gravity*, we aim to do just that.

In this book, Aadi is a young boy who grew up with unintentional but impactful parenting, rigid structures, and others' expectations that made him into a person with confusion, limiting beliefs, and self-doubt.

We truly believe that there is an Aadi in all of us. We all have different challenges that threaten to limit our potential. Some people are able to overcome these obstacles, while a majority of the young minds, bright and eager, are often lost. The common foundational challenges each of them face are the lack of the correct parental guidance that would have otherwise encouraged independence, curiosity, and resilience; an educational system that focuses on merit over growth; and excessive societal expectations and pressures that curb self-awareness.

As a result, in the race to chase the so-called success, unrealistic goals, they never got the time and opportunity to learn crucial life skills, such as problem-solving, emotional intelligence, and critical thinking, and never had the support to explore and discover their true potential. Reaching out to all those young individuals who have all this while felt unheard, unseen, or misunderstood and helping them through the story of Aadi has been our inspiration to write *Defy Your Gravity.*

The powerful narrative of Aadi's transformative journey – his challenges and triumphs – will surely strike a chord with you emotionally and will stay with you forever, influencing your choices, actions, and contributing to your growth, thereby becoming your transformative guide to rewrite your stars and *Defy Your Gravity.*

At the end of Aadi's story, we introduce Priti's real-life journey, showing how overcoming obstacles isn't just a fictional narrative but a reality many individuals face. While Aadi's struggles reflect the internal battles of self-doubt, frustration, and disappointments that many youth experience, Priti's story gives that battle a tangible face. Her triumph against all odds serves as proof that with the right mindset, perseverance, and values, real change is possible. Together, Aadi's fictional journey and Priti's real-world success offer powerful examples of how self-belief, resilience, and support can help anyone *Defy their Gravity.*

The Why: Why Should I Read This Book?

The relatable stories and life lessons in *Defy Your Gravity* will surely help you overcome self-doubt, fear, and negative beliefs while enabling you to recognize your potential and embark on an inspiring journey of *transforming your transformation.*

The What: What Will I Get From Reading This Book?

There's nothing in this book that you might not have known prior to reading it. However, its engaging narrative with practical examples backed by real-life instances of people who have defied their gravity will surely inspire you to embark on your journey of defiance, for personal growth, healing, and self-discovery.

At the end of each chapter, you'll find fun, thought-provoking activities that engage your mind and offer a moment of reflection along with suggesting the action steps for experiencing tangible results. For drawing maximum benefit, we urge you to attempt all these exercises that are backed by science and psychology before diving into the next chapter.

The How: How Should I Read This Book?

To get the most from **Defy Your Gravity,** read with curiosity and openness. Immerse yourself in Aadi's journey and reflect on how his experiences relate to your own. Take your time with each chapter. Attempt all the Reflection questions and action steps therein. After finishing each chapter, jot down your progress in the *'Progress Tracker'* given right after the Preface.

Revisit sections that resonate with you and use **Annexure G** to stack your reflections, thoughts, and anything you find important while reading. Treat this book both as a narrative journey and a personal toolkit for growth.

The Who: Who Is This Book For?

'Defy Your Gravity' is written for everyone, but especially for parents and the youth who feel lost in today's complex, competitive world. It's for those who think they've failed, for those burdened by societal pressures, and for anyone who's ever felt like giving up. We hope that this book inspires you to take ownership of your life and find your deeper purpose. A purpose that is compelling enough to enable you to rise above your challenges, and embrace your potential, thereby helping you in *'Branding Your Own Growth.'*

Welcome to your journey of defiance.
Let's rise together.

PROGRESS TRACKER

How to Use This Tracker

1. **Set Your Goals:** At the end of each chapter, take a moment to jot down your thoughts, feelings, and any insights you gained, write down what you hope to learn or achieve from that chapter.

2. **Challenges:** Figure out the challenges you foresee in achieving the identified goals for each chapter.

3. **Action Steps:** Define clearly, how you plan to rise above these challenges and Defy Your Gravity!

4. **Progress Check-Ins:** Depending on the timeline you set for achieving each of the identified goals, review your progress.

5. **Celebrate Achievements:** Don't forget to celebrate small victories along the way!

S.No	CHAPTER	GOALS	CHALLENGES	ACTION STEPS	COMPLETION DATE
1					
2					
3					
4					
5					
6					

S.No	CHAPTER	GOALS	CHALLENGES	ACTION STEPS	COMPLETION DATE
7					
8					
9					
10					
11					
12					
13					

S.No	CHAPTER	GOALS	CHALLENGES	ACTION STEPS	COMPLETION DATE
14					
15					
16					
17					
18					

By maintaining this tracker after every chapter, you will find yourself at the end of the book with a wonderful compilation of thoughts that resonate with you, as a ready-reckoner for the future.

ACKNOWLEDGMENT

At the very outset, we would like to tender our heartfelt gratitude to our God almighty, our Supreme Father. Your divine help has been the source of our inspiration and our strength while writing every single word. We pray for your continued grace and guidance.

We are deeply grateful to our late parents and grandparents, Ved Prakash Modi, Nirmal Modi, Dr. G.D. Goel, and Shanti Goel, whose teachings and values continue to guide us every day. Their wisdom, strong moral values, and their power of resilience – the ability to not just bounce back after challenges but to in fact grow through adversity – are all woven into the very fabric of this book.

This book would not have been possible without the continuous encouragement and feedback from Nitin, you're the world's best husband and father.

Our family—Aman, Nidhi, Varun, Arti, Meher, Dr. Amit, Dr. Ruchi, Navin, and Teena—we are so fortunate to have each one of you in our lives and for being our unconditional cheerleaders. Thank you for always being there for us.

A heartfelt thank you to Priti, a warrior, artist, choreographer, and a three-time finalist of the 'IGT', India's Got Talent Show, for generously sharing her incredible life journey with us. We are blessed to have found you. Your story completely validates our belief in the concept of *Defy Your Gravity*. We're forever indebted to you for sharing your story unconditionally, with utmost transparency and with the sole objective of inspiring and empowering young individuals and parents.

To everyone who has been a part of this journey, thank you. We are forever grateful for your contributions, big or small.

Sharing My Story

*Have you ever stopped to wonder how the stories
you tell yourself shape the person you become?*

I certainly didn't, until recently when my mother made me realize how deeply my negative self-talk had woven internal stories of inhibition, self-doubt, fear, and expectations, which had made inroads into my subconscious, pushing me into a stuck state, holding me back, and making me believe I was someone that 'I wasn't'.

As a kid, I was the complete opposite. I was fearless, forever happy, and an explorer. I viewed the world as full of endless possibilities. But somewhere along the way, I lost that version of myself. And now, at 23, here I am, unsure of who I am or what I'm supposed to be.

MAA

Connected by Love, Guided by Spirit.

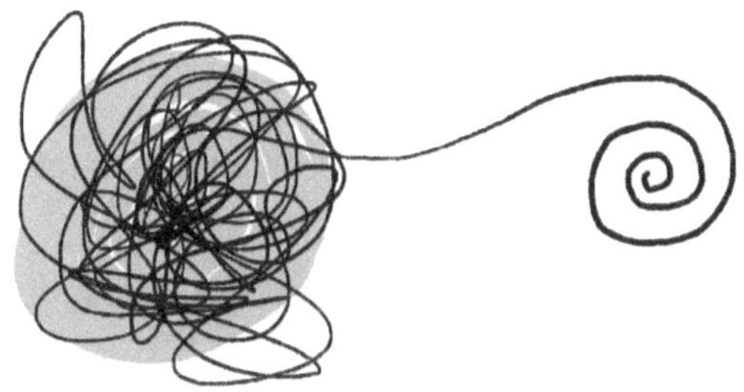

Spring has always been my favorite time of the year. I vividly remember vibrant flowers of different hues shining in the bright sunlight, gentle breezes, and the earthy scent, together made all those moments truly magical, showcasing the pure beauty of Mother Nature.

It was the same part of the year. But today, something inside me felt different, and I couldn't appreciate any of this. Even my popular intoxicating smile seemed to have faded away, leaving me blank and devoid of happiness and cheer.

As I rang the doorbell frantically, my mother opened the door. Without greeting her, I rushed straight into my room, giving her absolutely no chance to ask me anything. Upon entering the room, I kicked off my shoes, loosened my tie, and curled up in my bed. I felt terribly broken inside, almost lifeless.

I wondered what was happening to me. Why did I feel like this?

Just then, my father's voice pierced the silence. He sounded really angry and irritated as he yelled my name – "Aadi!" He had all the reasons to be upset. After all, it was a significant day for him as well. Khanna uncle, one of his closest friends, had arranged a job interview for me, and that's why my father had come home early, to ask me how my interview went this time, to hear all about it, hoping this time things would work in my favor, only to find me rush past him without even acknowledging his presence in the living room.

But was this such a tough guess? A question even worth asking? Wasn't the answer painfully obvious? After all, this wasn't my first interview. I had lost count of the number of times I had been rejected, and each time, I wished it would be the last, no more interviews, no more humiliation. Yet, this time, I too hoped that things would be different. Khanna uncle had been my one big HOPE.

But it wasn't different. The questions asked, the answers given, and the rejection that followed, it was all the same. Nothing had changed, and at that point, I was convinced nothing ever would. I knew this so well. Despite all my failures in the past, from my face-off with the devil that I saw in Math that forced me to choose the arts stream, to the rejection letters from prestigious colleges that further shattered my dreams. My first job, with its pathetic pay and a 30-mile commute each way, was bad enough. But it was the cruelty of my boss, Mr. Anant, who made each day so unbearable that I quit in a huff, without a plan, just desperate to escape.

Now, this endless search for a job felt like it was suffocating me, leaving me disappointed and frustrated. It had been months since I had caged myself in a self-imposed cocoon, no friends, no social life, and no one to share my pain with. *'Is this life even worth living?'* I wondered!

Just then, I heard a knock on the door. Before I could pretend to be asleep, my mother was already halfway across the room, carrying a tray of dinner.

"Maa, I don't need anything. I just want to sleep," I murmured, slipping under my blanket, pretending I was very sleepy. But mothers never give up easily, do they?

As she persisted, I finally snapped, "Why are you bothering me, Maa?" I shouted in frustration. "I'm a failure. I've accomplished nothing. I couldn't make Dad proud with a government job, nor could I fulfill your dream of becoming a doctor. My past has been difficult, my present is a mess, and my future is doomed." I buried myself under the bedsheet, crying bitterly, feeling ashamed for taking it out on her.

While I was hoping for her usual comforting and warm hug, her voice cut through the air, firm and almost startling. "That's the problem with your career. What's wrong with YOU?" she asked, and in that moment, it felt as though someone had poured cold water over my burning frustration. I instantly calmed down. How had she managed to pinpoint the very heart of my struggle, my real problem?

That was MAA, my Mom!

The one who sees into the depths of my being.

Meri Atma ki Antaryami
The keeper of my soul

She's my guide, my confidante, my unwavering companion, from the very first step I took as Aadi to the last mile of my journey. She doesn't just understand me, she knows me, inside and out.

"Your greatest failure is not the end;
it's the beginning of something far
greater, if you're willing to see it."

Dear Readers,

Mindfulness can help you stay grounded during life's challenges. Here are a few simple practices to get started:

1. **Deep Breathing:** 5 minutes a day focus on your breathing. Breathe in deeply for 5 seconds, hold for 5, and exhale for 5. Feel your body relax with each breath.

2. **Gratitude Journal:** Before retiring to bed daily, write down three things you are grateful for. This shifts your focus from problems to positivity.

3. **Body Scan:** Before retiring to bed, lie down straight, close your eyes and mentally scan your body from head to toe. Acknowledge any tension, and release it as you breathe out.

4. **Observe, Don't React:** The next time something stressful happens, take a moment to pause. Observe your thoughts, feelings, and body sensations without reacting immediately. Then respond calmly.

Mindfulness isn't about removing stress – it's about handling it with grace.

Reflection Question:

Think about a moment in your recent past when you felt overwhelmed or stressed. How did you respond to it, and at that time, what thoughts were running through your mind? How would practicing mindfulness have changed your experience at that moment?

Action Step:

Next time that you feel overwhelmed, take 60 seconds to pause, close your eyes, and take deep breaths. Focus on your breathing, letting go of all the racing thoughts. How does this change your reaction to stress?

02

SHATTERING ILLUSIONS: A PARENTING REALITY CHECK

In a split second, memories of the past came rushing back, how I always saw Maa engrossed in endless household chores. I used to think, given her years of teaching in college, what could she have possibly known about planning a career in the corporate world? After all, my desi Maa was the one spoiling me with delicious, mouth-watering dishes, taking care of our clothes, the laundry, the house… the list was endless.

"Aadi!" her gentle voice broke my reverie. "What are you thinking? Where have you drifted? Aadi, answer me, what's wrong?"

It was as though time had seized. I found no words, and my emotions were locked away. I stood there, staring at her, overwhelmed with gratitude. In that moment, and for a change, I realized my soul had found its true companion. There was someone who understood me more deeply than I understood myself.

"Yes, Aadi, I'm waiting," Maa said softly, her patience unwavering.

"Maa, I'm scared. If I open up, you might tell Dad, and then both of you will be upset. Things will just get worse, so let me deal with it on my own," I replied, my frustration barely contained.

"Handle what, Aadi?" she asked gently. "We're in this together. I'm your mother. No one in this world cares more about you than Dad and me. You can share whatever is on your mind. And Aadi, I'm not talking to you just because you're upset today. I've been wanting to sit with you and really understand the root of what's troubling you. I know that not getting a job isn't the real issue. Am I missing something? There's definitely something deeper, and together, let both of us figure it out."

Her words struck a chord deep inside me. Her reassuring words made me feel that she understood what I was going through. I felt connected to her, and suddenly it became so much easier to vent out my inner feelings.

Gaining courage, I slowly said, "Maa, nowadays, I feel both you and Dad don't love me anymore."

Shocked and concerned, both at the same time, she said, "What makes you think that, Aadi? We have only two children to care for, and we love both of you equally. Since when have you been feeling this way?"

"If you both love me, then why do I always feel like I'm never good enough? You've always compared me to Bhai, always making decisions about what's best for me without asking what I want. I never got a say in my own life. You've never taken the time to listen to me patiently, except for now, which is something rare. All that you both talk to me about is your to-do prescription list, things I have to do. Get up, take a bath, clean your room, study, work, sleep… If it weren't for these instructions, we'd probably never talk at all. That's all we ever talk about!"

I felt really sad after saying all of that, but something about today was different. Maa's question: "What's wrong with you, Aadi?" had struck deep enough for me to spill out the truth. The problem wasn't my job, my career, or even my luck, it went much deeper.

As if suddenly realizing something, she said, "Aadi, we've only ever wanted the best for you, to protect you from the mistakes we made. We tell you what to do because we believe it's for your own good. Who else would tell you these things if not us? Your Dad and I went through so many struggles early in life, and we don't want you and Bhai to go through that. We want to teach you the right things so you don't have to learn them the hard way by making avoidable mistakes. Is that so wrong, Aadi?"

Aadi didn't need to know the whole path

He just needed to take one action

"Maa, I know your intentions were always good," I replied, "but imagine what I must have felt as a 5-year-old, constantly hearing instructions and criticisms. Do you remember your early morning wake-up calls? 'Get up! You're too lazy! At this rate, you won't achieve anything in life!' That's not exactly a motivating start to anyone's day."

"Aadi, can't you see those mornings were chaotic for everyone? We all had to leave at the same time. I had to cook, pack lunches, prepare breakfast, handle other chores, and still get ready for the office. There was so little time, and your sluggish responses always made me rush!" Maa explained, sounding exasperated.

"I know, Maa, but I was too small for all that regimentation. Your repeated fault findings left an imprint on me. And over time, I started believing them. Now, I'm at a point where I've set this subconscious bar for myself. Even when I know I'm procrastinating or being lazy, I can't seem to break the cycle. It's as if hearing it all my life has convinced me that's who I am: lazy, indecisive, unorganized, underconfident, and always trying to please others. I'm so focused on what others think of me that I can't even figure out what I want for myself. You've pushed me so hard, Maa, and without realizing it, you both have only focused on your version of success. I'm terrified of disappointing you!" And this time, I couldn't hold back the tears.

"Oh, no Aadi! Is that what you've been thinking all along? I hadn't considered it that way at all," her voice choked. "Aadi, both your Dad and I have always wanted you to be successful and confident. But, perhaps we didn't let you explore, experiment, and make your own choices. Maybe we were just being overprotective as we didn't want you to make the same mistakes and fail. And without realizing, we've made things painful for you." I could see the genuine realization wash over her face as she hugged me tightly, her words heavy with meaning.

"I don't know... I just don't want to disappoint you again. It feels like everything I do is wrong. I feel like a total failure... I feel lost," I confessed, crying.

After a long heart-to-heart talk, Maa was happy I had shared my feelings with her and that she finally knew what my real problem was. She realized that all this had led me to believe that all that mattered were milestones, goals, and success. She regretted not letting me experiment and learn from failing like I did as a kid.

"It's okay to mess up. Don't overthink and don't think too far. You may not know all the things right now, but trust me, you'll figure it out as you move ahead. What's important is to stay focused, and keep trying. Not all battles are won, right? You don't have to prove it to everybody. And remember, we'll support every decision that you take. We're standing right behind you. Don't worry about the outcomes." I nodded, her words resonating deeply within me, a palpable weight lifting off my shoulders.

> **Healing begins the moment we realize that growth requires letting go of the past.**

As if determined not to waste a single moment, and before I could realize, Maa gently dragged me to our favorite couch on the balcony.

Asking me to sit, she said, "Do you know that we all have an innocent child within us? As we grow up, our increasing curiosity and desires often lead us to forget that child and the valuable lessons we can learn from the innocence of the kids around us. Are you listening?"

"Kids? What do they have to do with problems concerning my life and career?" I asked, bewildered.

"Come, let me share with you the five most important and incredible lessons we can learn from children, including the lessons from our own childhood," she said, wrapping me in a comforting hug and urging me to listen. "Aadi, do you know how crucial it is for a newborn baby to cry right after birth?" she asked.

"Yes, to open up the vocal cords," I replied, eager to show off my knowledge.

"Exactly! When a baby enters the real world, it faces its first challenge: adapting to a completely new environment. The mother's womb is warm and safe, while the world outside is cold, unfamiliar, and daunting. Inside the womb, the baby doesn't need to use its lungs, but once it's born, it must breathe on its own, hence the first cry."

The cry of a newborn signifies so much. It's the first time the baby uses sound to express its emotions, it's the initial form of communication between the baby and its mother. The moment a newborn cries, it takes its first breath. From then on, the child learns to articulate its needs, crying for food, comfort, or for sleep. So, why do we forget that first natural emotion, that primal form of communication, *crying*?"

"So, are you telling me to become a crybaby at my age? Please, Maa, I'm not a baby anymore! I'm a 23-year-old adult!" I reacted a bit harshly.

"Aadi, when I say 'cry', I mean let your emotions flow! Share them with those you trust, those who understand and can help you cope. By expressing your pain, you find support that strengthens you to face your fears."

	New Born Baby	Adults
1st Challenge	Coming out of the warmth of the womb into a new outside world, unable to breathe without the mother's placenta	As we step out into the world of school, college, or office, it could be: • Lack of knowledge • Bullying in school or college • Poor grades • Comparison • Failure in Interviews • Lack of money
Action it takes	CRIES	Suffocate ourselves by not sharing our worries with our loved ones.
Result	Lungs start to function, and the loved ones rush to help	• This leads to more complicated situations. • Get frustrated, disappointed, and angry • Holds us back from improving.

Dear Readers,

As parents, we must empower our children through positive communication. Our words and actions shape our children's worldview. Here are some tips to enhance your communication with them:

1. **Active Listening:** Don't just hear your child – LISTEN.

   Give them your full attention and let them know their voice matters.

2. **Encourage Questions:** Allow your child to ask questions, even the most weird ones.

   This nurtures their curiosity and problem-solving skills.

3. **Replace Criticism with Constructive Feedback:** Instead of saying, "You always make mistakes," say, "I see you're trying. Let's work on this together."

4. **Express Emotions with Words:** Teach your child to express their emotions through words. This will help them manage their feelings instead of acting out.

   When you feel upset, tell me what's bothering you instead of getting angry. For example, you can say, 'I feel sad because…' or 'I feel frustrated when…'

   Encourage them to label emotions like 'happy', 'sad', or 'frustrated', and guide them in describing what they're feeling in specific situations. Over time, this helps them manage their emotions by talking about their feelings rather than reacting impulsively.

5. **Be their Cheerleader, Not just a Guide:** Encourage them to explore, even if they stumble. Celebrate their effort, not just the result.

Reflection Question:

Do you think it's important to teach our children to make their own decisions?

Think about all the decisions that you make for your child without involving him or her. What is the reason and your motivation behind that choice? Now, out of these, select a few decisions that you think can be left to them to make on their own. How well are your kids likely to handle it? Do you think letting them make their own choices can boost their confidence and growth?

Action Step:

- To start with, choose any one decision – that you would normally make for your child. For example, deciding what they wear, how they organize their study time, or what activities they engage in.

- For the next week, leave it to them to make their informed choices. You may guide them through the process if and when needed.

- Ask them how they feel about the options and which choices would make them the happiest or most comfortable.

- Reflect afterward on how this empowered them and how you felt about letting go of control.

03

PARENTING WITH PURPOSE

Guiding, Not Controlling

I f you'd asked me a few years ago what parenting was, I would have said it's all about rules, discipline, and ensuring you don't mess up. That's what I'd always experienced, a constant need to live up to expectations, to be good enough, and to follow the path my parents set out for me. But as I've come to realize, parenting is about so much more than that.

Looking back now, I understand something I didn't before: no one loves you more than your parents. No one wants your happiness more, even when it doesn't always seem that way.

And since they only act out of love and care, they try to protect us from the big bad world outside our safe homes. They might become overprotective, unintentionally holding us back, and might make some mistakes too, but considering that they are humans, we must not judge them. Sure, it may seem like a burden at times, but that love is the greatest gift.

Like all other parents, my parents too raised me with care, compassion, and the hope that I would succeed. Their approach might not have aligned with what I deserved, but when they realized I was struggling, that I wasn't the person I could be, they opened up, listened, admitted to whatever went wrong, became receptive to change, and allowed me to grow. That's what changed everything. They didn't just love me, they showed that they were willing to learn with me.

And that's what being a parent is all about, evolving along with your child, giving them the freedom to find their own way while being their steady support. I wasn't just a child who needed guidance–I became someone who needed room to breathe, to make mistakes, and to get back up again.

The key is communication, being open enough as children to express what we need, and for parents to be receptive enough to hear us without judgment. That's when real growth begins.

Parenting is all about trust. It's about open and effective communication. Instead of exercising excessive control, partner with them in their journey and know when to step in and when to step back. And most importantly, it's about letting your child become who they are, not who you want them to be.

No matter the misunderstandings or difficulties, no one has your back like your parents. They might not always get it right, but their intentions are always grounded in love. And that's something I've learned to value more than anything.

Even in their imperfections, a parent's love remains the truest form of unconditional care.

04

THE JOY WITHIN

Mastering Your Inner Voice

During the last few days that I'd been having heart-to-heart conversations with Mom, I had started feeling very relaxed. That feeling of being heard and understood had helped strengthen our bond even more.

"Your thoughts shape your reality; by reframing them, you hold the power to transform your world."

Just when I was engrossed in my happy thoughts, Maa entered my room and gave me a big tight hug. In that moment, I wished time would stand still, allowing me to linger in her loving arms, free from all my worries.

"What are your needs, Aadi? What would make you truly happy in life?"

"Mom, I thought you already knew!" I replied, exasperated.

"Aadi, I genuinely want you to tell me," Maa insisted.

"Mom, I need a successful career, a high-paying job, a house of my own, and a big car. I want to go on a world tour, buy designer clothes, and dine in five-star restaurants! The list is endless." A sly smile crept across my face; I could almost feel myself embarking on a dream adventure.

"That's nice to hear, Aadi! But those are likely the wishes of many people. They don't necessarily equate to what you truly need for a happy life," Maa responded gently.

"Now, close your eyes and think about the basic needs of an infant. What does a newborn truly require to be happy?" she gently urged.

"Mom, I'm not a newborn baby who can survive on just food and sleep! Life doesn't work that way, and you know it! If that were enough, why would any of us bother with studying, chasing good grades, or trying to get into top schools and colleges? To live in this world, it's about more than just '*Roti, Kapda, aur Makaan*'—food, clothing, and shelter—if that's where you're headed!" I retorted.

"Aadi, there's a clear line between ambition, productivity, and getting trapped in the rat race. It's healthy to be ambitious, to strive for your best, and unlock your potential. The trouble begins when we start expecting too much from ourselves, especially when we compare ourselves with others and get caught in that endless race. That isn't sustainable. First, understand what genuinely makes you happy. Recognize your strengths, accept your limitations, and aim to give your best, without losing sight of who you are.

Happiness, in its purest form, is a natural gift, as minimal as the joy a newborn feels. Every baby has four basic needs: food, sleep, a clean diaper, and human connection for comfort. As we grow, our desires become more varied—different foods, toys, entertainment, relationships—and that's okay! What's *not* okay is letting the absence of these things make us feel disheartened or defeated.

Appreciate everything you achieve and cherish even the smallest blessings. Anything beyond life's essentials should inspire humility and gratitude. Instead of focusing on what you lack, take meaningful steps toward your dreams. I learned that true happiness comes from expecting less and staying purpose-driven. When you're genuinely happy, your body releases positive hormones, naturally motivating growth and excellence.

This can happen only when you:

- Appreciate everything you have.

- Strive to reach your full potential while keeping expectations minimal.

- Grow without getting trapped in the rat race.

- Choose happiness and stay motivated, respecting and learning from your own decisions," she said.

"But Mom, that's easier said than done. I can lower my expectations to the bare minimum and try to avoid getting caught up in the rat race, but what happens when I still fail? That can be really disheartening."

"Aadi, I'm getting to that. But for now, do you agree it's beneficial to share your emotions and seek help when needed? Focus on your basic needs, cultivate gratitude for what you have, and make an effort to stay happy and positive while pursuing your dreams. How? We'll discuss that in more detail soon."

Somewhere inside me, I could feel that my journey toward self-empowerment had started and today seemed to be that one significant turning point that would probably reshape the way I'd been viewing my challenges for so long. Today, my mother introduced me to new ways of approaching my challenges, drawing on techniques like *reframing* through *Neuro-Linguistic Programming (NLP)*.

I figured out the reasons why my internal dialogue or self-talk was full of negative phrases like:

"I'm not good enough."

"I always fail."

"My life will never get better."

The reason being, all through my growing up years, I suffered due to my perception of failure, years of feeling compared to my older brother, enduring a strict upbringing, and facing setbacks in my education and career. I somehow believed my past mistakes define me to be a person with all the flaws and limitations.

So my mom encouraged me to look inwards, analyze myself through certain self-awareness exercises, and most importantly shift my perspective about how I viewed myself. To do this, I had to change the flow of my thoughts. I had to change patterns that directed my thinking.

I was puzzled. "What do you mean, Maa? I can't change the fact that I've failed, over and over."

My mother smiled softly and replied, "What if I told you that you haven't failed at all? Instead, you've been gathering valuable lessons. Let's explore something called reframing, together."

She explained to me that reframing is about changing the meaning of what happens to us. She said, "The events in our life don't come with built-in meaning, we assign meaning to them. And that means we can choose a different meaning, one that empowers us instead of weighing us down."

She gave me an example from my own life.

"You keep saying that you've failed because you didn't get into the college you wanted. But what if we looked at that same event from a different angle? What if this wasn't a failure but a learning experience?"

I frowned. "How is not getting into a college a learning experience?"

"Every challenge, every setback in life presents two options for us to choose from. One, accept, analyze and plan the corrective effort to fully utilize the opportunity at hand. The other option is to get terribly affected by the setback and lose faith in yourself. Feeling emotionally hurt is not bad, provided you are able to bounce back with a stronger resolve.

So, when you did not get admission to the college of your choice, initially you did feel disappointed but now if you reflect on it, you'd realize the important lessons it taught you – that of adaptability and resilience. These are valuable life skills that would help you both professionally and personally. It's a chance to pause, reflect, and figure out what you really want. Maybe it's pushing you to explore other opportunities or paths you hadn't considered before. Instead of seeing it as a failure, think of it as a stepping stone, a moment to redirect your energy and focus toward something that might be an even better fit for you. Every setback is an opportunity to grow stronger and wiser, and this one is no different. Isn't that valuable?"

Slowly, I began to see what my mother was trying to show me. I realized that not getting into my dream college had indeed pushed me to reflect on what I really wanted, instead of following a path laid out for me by others.

Next, my mother asked me about my experience with my first job, which had left me feeling defeated and worthless.

"Let's reframe this too," she suggested. "You keep saying that you quit because you weren't capable. That you couldn't deal with your boss. But what else could this mean? Considering the fact that you didn't quit in a huff. Could it mean that you did try to give it your best, tolerated long enough beyond your capacity and that, in fact, you were wise enough to walk away from a toxic environment?"

I paused. I hadn't thought of it like that. I had only seen my decision to leave as a sign of weakness.

My mother continued, "By leaving that job, you showed incredible strength. You stood up for yourself. You recognized that staying would have been damaging to your mental health. That's not failure, Aadi, that's empowerment."

For the first time, I felt liberated from guilt. I hadn't failed by quitting. I had protected my well-being.

"The more you continue to practice reframing, the more your internal dialogue will begin to shift. Instead of repeating negative beliefs, start asking yourself reframing questions:

'What can I learn from this?'

'How does this challenge help me grow?'

'What's another way to see this situation?'

In the beginning, consciously reframe your thoughts and eventually you will find yourself free of negative thinking. Reframe:

From: 'I'm a failure.'

To: 'I am learning from every experience, and I am growing stronger.'

Trust me and try this for a few weeks in other areas of your life. This time, when anyone offers you a piece of unsolicited advice that frustrates you, simply reframe your thoughts:

'He's not trying to control me. He's trying to help in the only way he knows how.'

When you think of the recent rejections from job interviews, instead of giving up, reframe:

'This isn't the end. Every rejection brings me closer to the right opportunity.'

With each reframe, you'll grow more resilient. No longer will you feel trapped by your circumstances. Instead, you will see every challenge as a stepping stone toward your growth. With continued practice, you'll find your overall perspective on life will soon begin to change. You will stop feeling like a victim of your circumstances. Instead, you will start seeing yourself as the author of your own story. The events that once seemed like failures to you will become pivotal moments of learning and growth."

Today, my mother taught me the most valuable lesson of all: life is not about what happens to you, but how you interpret it.

"What's on your mind, Aadi? Does this make sense to you? Cheer up! It's time to let go of negative self-talk. Apply for jobs with renewed confidence, explore your passions, and view each day as a fresh opportunity to rewrite your story."

Mom's words began to declutter my mind of negative influences, and I felt eager to discover what more was to unfold.

Dear Readers,

Here's an exercise that will help reduce mental clutter and bring your focus to the present, making you more mindful and engaged before you start reading the next chapter.

The 5-4-3-2-1 Grounding Exercise

How to do it:

- 5 things: Look around and name five things you can see.
- 4 things: Touch four things around you and notice their texture
- 3 things: Listen for three sounds in your environment.
- 2 things: Identify two distinct smells
- 1 thing: Take a moment to taste something (even if it's just noticing the taste in your mouth)

Scientific Basis: Grounding techniques have been proven to reduce anxiety, increase mindfulness, and improve focus. This method anchors the mind to the present, creating a more relaxed and concentrated state.

Fun Element: Get creative! Try to find things that are unusual or out of the ordinary in your surroundings.

Reflective Question:

Think about a situation where you felt disappointed or negative recently. How did your internal dialogue shape your emotional response? How could you have reframed that situation to focus on possibilities rather than problems?

Action Step:

For the next 7 days, practice reframing your internal dialogue:

So, when you encounter a negative situation, pause and consciously identify the language you are using in your internal dialogue.

Then, ask yourself, "How can I reframe this thought to see a positive or an opportunity here?" For example, if you're thinking, "This is too hard, I can't do it," reframe it as, "This is challenging, but it's helping me grow and learn."

Write down the old thought and your new reframed thought each day. After a week, reflect on how this shift in language affected your mood, resilience, and ability to remain positive.

05

SETTING YOUR HAPPINESS COMPASS

Navigating Life with Joyful Anchors

I'd started reflecting more on my past situations and reframing surely helped me shift my perspectives and view my problems with a whole new, fresh and positive outlook. But, what if I face the same situation again? Would I be able to control my emotional responses or be back to my vulnerable self? Engrossed in these thoughts, I was submerged in my past and that's when I heard a knock on my door, saw my mom entering the room, and I was pulled back into my present.

"Aadi, I have a confession to make," said Maa.

"A confession? What is it, Maa?" I sat up straight after hearing these words as she stood up to open an old cabinet in the room. She pulled out an album, and my excitement dipped when I realized it was just my childhood album, filled with memories from the day I was born.

"Before you came into our lives, like most couples, we started out with very little. Despite that, we had many hopes and dreams. But, as you know, not all dreams come true," she said. "My biggest confession is this: Aadi, you have been my greatest teacher in life. You've taught me some of life's most valuable lessons and have shaped me into the strong, humble, and grounded person that I am today."

"Me? How can that be, Maa? I don't feel strong at all."

"Aadi, from the moment you were born, I had the chance to watch you as a baby, up close. That experience made me realize how wonderfully nature has given us the instincts to grow, face challenges, and evolve. Yes, evolve! If we apply the lessons from a baby's journey to our daily lives, we can find happiness like the happiest child on this planet. Do you want to hear more about what I learned from you as a baby?" Her eyes sparkled with joy.

"Yes, Maa. I agree that children are incredibly innocent and show genuine emotions. What I've liked the best about them is they just don't seem to give up! I remember *Chetan*, my cousin, persisting to learn to crawl. No fall could stop him; he just kept trying until the day he finally stood up and started walking. It's super cute and truly inspiring!" I said, lovingly.

"Wow! That's an amazing observation, Aadi," she said, smiling while looking for her spectacles, which often go missing in our house. "Shall we do a quick rapid-fire round? I'll mention some traits of babies, and you can guess the valuable lessons we can learn from them," she suggested.

"Sure! Let's start," I replied with conviction.

"I'll show you some pictures from this album. Pay attention to what you're doing in each one, then figure out a lesson that you, I, and all adults can use to tackle our complex problems in simple ways!"

"Look at this picture. You can see yourself happily playing with your teether! But do you know the story behind this picture?" she asked.

It sounded interesting as we had never discussed the stories behind my childhood pictures ever before.

"Well, just the night before, you had a terrible stomach ache, or at least that's what we thought. You howled the whole night, and your dad and I stayed up trying everything we could: gripe water, milk, heeng water, and rocking you around the entire house, but nothing worked. And look at you the next morning! What do you take away from this?"

"That's unbelievable, Maa! Did I cause you that much trouble? I'm so sorry!" I said, grateful for everything she had done for me.

"The one lesson I can think of is to start every new day on a fresh note. If I'm not wrong, it means not to carry yesterday's baggage into today, right, Maa?" I asked.

"Yes, absolutely bang on! Every new day brings new opportunities! This mindset sets a positive tone for life. From you, I've learned to wake up with a smile, eager to practice and learn new skills. Aadi, kids are like little emotional experts – they feel their feelings intensely and aren't shy about expressing them. By observing kids and toddlers keenly, we can learn some of the most valuable life lessons about recognizing and managing our own emotions.

Just the way toddlers fall, cry for a moment, and then completely forget about it when something fun catches their attention, like a toy or someone making a silly face, is a perfect example of a concept called *'State management'*.

"Happiness is not a destination; it's a compass guiding you through life's storms, anchored by moments of joy."

Adults can also tap into this ability, though it may take a bit more conscious effort. Say, for example, work has left you feeling tense. You can redirect that feeling—similar to the way children do—by practicing a few simple techniques: try deep breathing, picture a peaceful place, or use a practiced physical anchor, such as pressing your fingers together, to bring about calm. By doing so, you can move from tension to a state of focus or relaxation, just as children naturally shift from one emotion to another, like going from tears to laughter.

One's ability to shift emotional states, known as 'state flexibility', is a superpower when it comes to handling challenges and maintaining composure.

There's a very beautiful natural coping mechanism behind this. You know, kids naturally link simple things, like a favorite toy or a familiar routine, to positive emotions. Like we just discussed how a child might feel instantly calm and happy when they hold their favorite stuffed animal or feel excited when they hear a specific song associated with playtime. These positive associations happen effortlessly in their world, don't they?

We can use and adopt this idea through an NLP technique called anchoring. Anchoring helps us build positive emotional associations in a purposeful manner. By linking a particular touch, sound, or word to a specific emotional state—like calmness or confidence—we can bring up that feeling whenever it's needed. This technique lets us access desired emotions on demand by connecting them to chosen cues.

For example, if you get nervous before giving a presentation, you can create something called an 'anchor' (think of it like a secret code just for you). Choose a gesture, like gently touching your thumb and forefinger together. Now practice this gesture when you're feeling calm and relaxed, maybe after meditating or exercising. With practice, this gesture will remind your mind and body of that calm feeling.

In the future, when you're about to give a presentation and start feeling nervous, you can use the same gesture to bring back those relaxed feelings and stay calm.

Another example could be associating a favorite song or a power phrase with confidence. Imagine playing a specific upbeat song before heading into a meeting or interview. If you repeat this enough, eventually just hearing that song—even in your head—can trigger those confident feelings, helping you to step into the situation feeling empowered.

By using anchoring, we can train ourselves to respond more positively to situations that might otherwise feel stressful, just as kids naturally do with their toys or daily routines. It's a powerful way to take control of our emotional states and respond better to life's challenges! Are you ready for the next lesson?" Maa beamed, her enthusiasm infectious.

Reflective Question:

Think about a time when you felt particularly happy, strong, confident, or in control. What were the circumstances that led to that feeling? How can you recreate or access that same feeling in challenging situations?

Action Step:

For the Next Week, Practice 'Creating a Positive Anchor'.

Identify a specific positive experience from your past that made you feel empowered and happy (e.g., receiving praise, achieving a goal, or spending time with loved ones). Whenever you recall this memory, take a deep breath, close your eyes, relax, and focus on the feelings associated with that moment. Don't forget to wear your smile on your face! Then, choose a simple physical gesture, such as placing your hand over your heart or clenching your fist. Use this gesture while immersing yourself in the positive feelings of that experience.

The next time you face a challenge or feel overwhelmed, use this same gesture to trigger those positive feelings and boost your confidence.

Reflect on how this practice influences your emotional state throughout the week.

06

SETTING A HAPPY TONE FOR LIFE

How I Found My Happy Place

As I turned the pages, a flood of memories came rushing back, there I was, a little version of me, grinning, pulling funny faces, sulking one moment and then bouncing back with a smile.

I realized I'd completely forgotten how to bounce back from things like that.

Looking at those photos, it dawned on me that back then, as a baby, I didn't complicate things. If I was upset, I found a way to shake it off, whether it was a favorite toy or just changing the scene around me. I had my own little way of *'anchoring'* myself back to feeling good, even if I didn't know what that was called at the time.

Thanks to Maa, I learned I could still do this! I could set up my own anchors, little reminders or routines to pull myself out of any gloom. And it doesn't have to be complicated. Sometimes, it's just a favorite song, a moment of quiet, or even a deep breath to remind me I've been through tough times before and made it out okay.

Growing up isn't about forgetting those good vibes. It's about bringing those little tricks from childhood into the adult world, using them to stay grounded when life gets chaotic. That old album reminded me of how to find my balance again.

When I start feeling overwhelmed—like on a tough workday or during a stressful moment—I take a pause. I try to remember how, as a kid, I'd hold tight to anything that made me feel happy. Now, I've created my own ways to bring back that feeling. One thing I do is keep a playlist of songs from my carefree days. The moment I press play, something in my mind just shifts, like a light switch turning on.

Suddenly, I'm not just listening to music; I feel lighter, like I'm right back in those happy, simple days.

And I keep a photo of Mom and Dad in my wallet. Whenever stress hits, I pull it out and take a moment to hold it. It's a little reminder that it's okay to feel what I'm feeling, and it's fine to let it go.

By anchoring myself in those memories and emotions, I've learned to shift my mindset, pulling myself out of negativity and back into strength and hope. It's all about recreating that childlike wonder, finding joy in the little things, and giving myself permission to feel and heal.

Funny how those childhood lessons never really leave us; you just have to remember to tap into them.

The wisdom of our childhood is
like a treasure chest, waiting to be
unlocked; sometimes, all it takes is
a gentle reminder to dig deep and
rediscover its gems.

07

THE UNSTOPPABLE YOU!

Facing Your Challenges Head-On

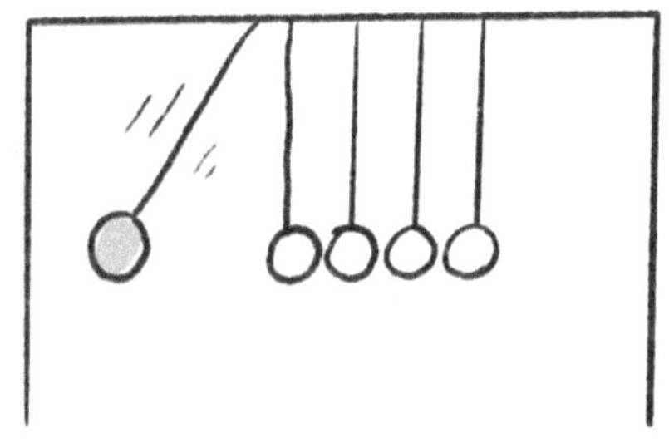

Small steps, when consistent create
Unstoppable Momentum

You know, growing up, I completely forgot how easy it was to change my mood. As a kid, I'd go from crying to laughing in a flash, no stress or overthinking like we do as adults. Life was just simpler back then. As I grew up, life became more about responsibilities, meeting expectations, and that nagging fear of making mistakes. But today, when Maa pulled out my childhood album, I realized how long it had been since I'd looked at it. Smiling, she picked out a picture and asked me to guess the story behind it. I leaned in, feeling a mix of curiosity and a bit of hesitation.

"What?! Am I trying to eat blades of grass? Ew! And what am I doing under that bush? Please, Maa! I hope that's not me!" I was embarrassed seeing the picture.

"Of course, that's you! While I was busy gardening, you crawled out of your pram and made your way straight to the bushes. You were munching on leaves, flowers, anything you could get your hands on. And the moment I turned and saw you making those crunching sounds with leaves, I simply couldn't stop laughing. Guess what lesson I learned that day?"

"Mom, are you saying I was a little explorer?" I laughed, trying to shake off the embarrassment.

"Yes, exactly my dear! Kids, in general, keep trying out new things without a second thought, even if it means getting a little messy or feeling hurt in the process," she paused and said in a thoughtful tone. "That curiosity, that openness to life, sadly Aadi, it's something we adults tend to let go of over time. But we really shouldn't."

Curiosity & Flexibility

"Kids are naturally curious and adaptable. If something doesn't go their way, they don't overthink it, they just move on and try something else.

That's behavioral flexibility, the ability to adapt and adjust when things don't work out as expected," Maa explained. Then she added with a smile, "When I married your dad, I was only 21, young and unprepared for so many things.

"I was scared to try anything new because I didn't want to fail. But that day, watching you, I learned a powerful mantra: step out of your comfort zone. Life isn't just about staying safe – it's about exploring, growing, and embracing every adventure that comes your way."

"You really think it's that easy, Maa? Just stepping out of your comfort zone?"

She nodded thoughtfully and told me that though failing is not always easy, it's worth it. "Failure is tough, Aadi, but it's not the end, it's actually a new beginning. Yes, you'll face challenges, but those challenges are what shape you. Every time you stumble, you learn something new, and that's how you grow. These challenges aren't there to stop you; they're there to make you stronger, wiser, and more resilient. Each setback builds your ability to handle whatever comes next. So, instead of seeing failure as something to avoid, think of it as a stepping stone toward becoming unstoppable. Every failure is simply a lesson in disguise."

I smiled, feeling the truth in her words. "So, what you're saying is… if I want to succeed, I need to stop worrying about the *'what ifs'* and just go for it?"

Modeling Success

Maa had a point. I'd always seen kids as learners, but maybe adults could learn just as much from them. Having watched my niece *Dhaar* grow up, I couldn't agree more that kids are curious, flexible, and brave enough to try new things without overthinking. That's what makes them such great problem-solvers. If I could just model that mindset—embracing challenges, staying curious, and being flexible—I could navigate my own life with the same kind of freedom I had back then. Maybe I didn't need to have everything figured out right now. I just needed to be open to learning, growing, and trying no matter what.

How about this? Why not jot down some things you've never tried because they made you feel uncomfortable? Or better yet, why not **list the challenges you feel you haven't been able to tackle?** Write them here on this page," she said, handing me a pen.

In a surprising turn, the thrill of jumping into this hands-on session with Maa stirred up a mix of excitement and curiosity in me. It felt like we were setting off on a shared journey, one where every step held the promise of fresh insights and growth. Embracing this moment with an open mind made me feel ready to push past my comfort zone and explore possibilities I hadn't dared to consider before.

"Maa, excuse my handwriting, but here I go!"

1. I've never been good at initiating small conversations with strangers or new colleagues. It just scares me.

2. As much as I would have wanted to, I've never been able to learn a new skill, whether professionally or even as a hobby. It just feels like too much effort.

3. I'm scared of applying to big companies or for big roles. I guess I'm afraid of the competition and the potential failures that might come with it.

4. I always hesitate to commit confidently, whether it's to deadlines at work, helping others, or similar tasks. I'm afraid that if I can't meet those expectations, miss deadlines, or fail to contribute enough, people will hold me accountable, point out my inefficiency, and blame me. As a result, I become overly cautious.

5. I also feel that I'm overly sensitive to feedback and tend to get defensive. Taking criticism is difficult for me, giving justifications with a closed mind has been my approach.

6. I'm always trying to please people. I know many of my friends and colleagues have strong opinions and are very expressive, but I'm constantly afraid that people will either get angry or judge me for my remarks. So, I end up trying to be 'goody-goody' with everyone all the time. More often than not, they see this as a weakness, and as a result, I've become very vulnerable.

7. I'm constantly trying to prove that I'm the best, but it doesn't work in my favor, and I end up staying stressed all the time.

8. I've lost my originality as an individual forever trying to prove that I'm the best. This more often than not leads me to unnecessary stress.

9. I shy away from making friends with smart and intelligent people even though I might have more knowledge than many of them. In fact, I always try not to hang around such people due to a lack of confidence and the lack of ability to showcase my knowledge.

10. I get troubled by work pressure and the pressure to perform. Why should I need you to comfort me Maa? Why am I unable to face my challenges without getting depressed, discouraged, or dejected? Why can't I be a self-motivator?

11. I aim for an easy road in life even though it might be less ambitious or less rewarding.

12. I'm not daring enough. Please Maa, shouldn't I be taking more risks at this time of my life? I feel that for sure.

13. I also feel I wasted my prime years of learning, age 12-21, watching TV, playing online games, and not cultivating good habits and discipline. Wish I had listened to you Maa.

14. I'm a little impulsive in making decisions. I simply lack patience.

15. Honestly speaking, Maa I wish I had cultivated the habit of reading. My communication and language skills would have been so much better.

16. I procrastinate a lot!

17. I am very shy. I fear people will be judging me.

"Great job, Aadi. Not many people are as aware of themselves as you are. Well done!" said Maa.

"Now tell me honestly, is it the first time you thought about all this, or was it very easy to jot down this list?"

"No, Maa, it wasn't easy by any means. I'd never given so much time to think about myself. Never. That's the reason it's taken me over an hour to make this close to a 20-point list. But I must confess that I do feel so much more relaxed after putting it all down." Maa was so happy to hear me say that.

Dear Readers,

It's always a great idea to reflect on where we stand and what lies ahead.

Would you like to attempt a small exercise? Ready! Think about yourself, and answer the following honestly.

1. What are my strengths? (Examples: Patience, Creativity, Communication)

2. What areas do I struggle with? (Examples: Self-doubt, Procrastination, Fear of failure)

3. How do I respond to challenges? (Do I face them or avoid them?)

4. What small steps can I take today to improve in any one area that I struggle with?

5. What is one thing I need to forgive myself for?

Take time to reflect on these answers.
Awareness is the first step to transformation.

08

FACING THE MIRROR

My Journey Through Challenges

Having discussed in detail with Maa and putting down a list of challenges was no less than looking at myself in the mirror. I had to confront myself to overcome these hurdles.

Let's start with *small talk*. When I first joined a new team, the thought of initiating conversations with colleagues made me feel like I was going to burst. I'd literally rehearse icebreakers in my head, but when the moment came, I'd feel paralyzed, just like a deer frozen in the glare of headlights. One day, I decided to change that. I made a pact with myself: just say "Hi!" to someone new every day. Sounds simple, right? But that simple greeting opened the door to more meaningful conversations. I learned that people appreciate a friendly smile and that I didn't need to be perfect; just genuine.

Now, about *learning new skills*, I realized I was creating a mountain out of a molehill. Here too, the fear of failure paralyzed me. Instead of trying to conquer everything at once, I picked one skill to focus on. I started small, like learning a few new recipes on weekends or experimenting with different art techniques online.

I discovered that breaking things down into bite-sized pieces made the learning process enjoyable rather than overwhelming. And guess what? I actually started to look forward to those moments!

Applying for jobs at big companies felt like a whole different challenge. I would freak myself out thinking, *'What if I don't get picked?'* But then I had this lightbulb moment: every successful person has faced rejection at some point.

So, I decided to change how I looked at things. I treated each application like a chance to practice, focusing on what I could learn from the experience instead of just worrying about the outcome. That shift in mindset made a huge difference.

The Growth Journey

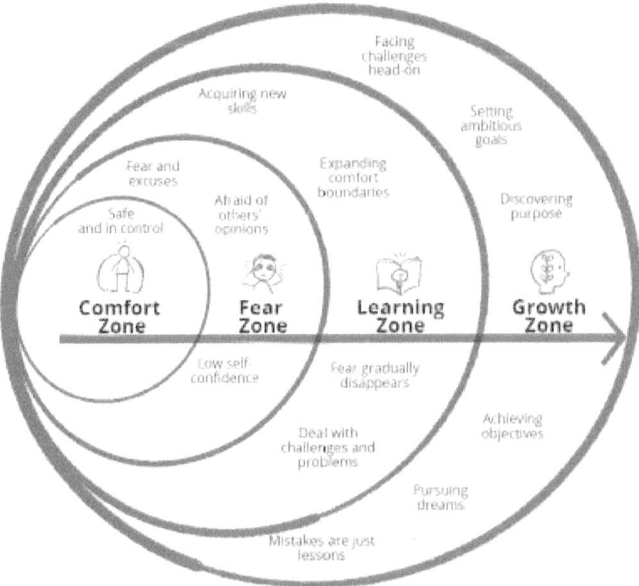

The ***pressure of deadlines and commitments*** was suffocating. I often hesitated to commit, fearing I wouldn't live up to expectations. To tackle this, I started practicing self-compassion. I realized it's okay to ask for help when I need it. If I couldn't meet a deadline, I'd communicate early, explaining my situation instead of letting anxiety consume me.

Receiving ***feedback was another hurdle***. I was defensive, always ready to justify myself. I began reminding myself that feedback is an opportunity for growth. Instead of viewing it as criticism, I learned to take a step back, listen, and separate my self-worth from my work. This approach not only helped me accept criticism but also improved my performance over time.

Pleasing everyone? Guilty as charged. I often felt like a doormat, thinking that if I kept everyone happy, I'd avoid conflict. But that only drained me. I learned it's okay to have my own opinions and stand by them. I started expressing myself in small doses, practicing being assertive without feeling aggressive.

As for making ***friends with smart people***, I realized I was letting my insecurities dictate my choices. I actively sought out discussions with those I admired. To my surprise, I discovered they also had their vulnerabilities! Connecting with them helped me appreciate my own knowledge and that I had something valuable to contribute.

Dealing with pressures—whether from work or self-imposed—was tough. Instead of seeking external validation, I started to focus inward. I learned that self-motivation comes from setting small, achievable goals and celebrating those wins, no matter how minor. It's a work in progress, but I'm learning to comfort myself, instead of relying on others.

Then there was that feeling of having ***wasted time during my formative years***. Yeah, I spent a lot of time on TV and games, but it's never too late to start cultivating good habits. I took up reading. I picked topics that genuinely interested me, and soon I was devouring books. My communication skills improved, and I found myself more engaged in conversations.

Procrastination? It's like an old buddy whom I just can't shake off. But I've started tackling it with time management techniques. I set timers for focused work sessions, breaking tasks into manageable chunks. The key is to just start; once I begin, momentum takes over.

Lastly, my **shyness**. I had to embrace the fact that being '*bindas*' (carefree) doesn't mean being reckless. I practiced stepping out of my comfort zone little by little. Every small risk, whether striking up a conversation or sharing an idea in a meeting, made me realize that the fear of judgment is often far worse than the reality.

By the end of this self-reflection, I felt a sense of relief and empowerment. Sure, I still have a long way to go, but recognizing these challenges and taking actionable steps to overcome them has been the first crucial step in my journey. With each small victory, I'm beginning to find my voice and the strength to become the person I aspire to be.

09

FEELINGS 101

Understanding What's Happening in Your Heart

When life feels like a dead end...

a single realization can spark a ~NEW~ BEGINNING

"**A**adi, remember how you always loved hearing stories from *Naani* and *Daadi* Ma?"

"Yes, Maa! They were such strong women. If I could inherit even 1% of their spirit, I'd consider myself successful. I'm truly proud of my grandparents."

"Stories like '*The Ants and the Elephant*,' '*The Ugly Duckling*,' '*The Boy Who Cried Wolf*,' '*The Grasshopper and the Ants*,' '*The Grapes and The Fox*,' '*Lazy John*,' '*The Thirsty Crow*,' and '*The Tortoise and the Hare*' each impart important life lessons. They teach us to nurture a positive mindset. Cultivating mental strength helps us understand ourselves, face challenges with resilience, and build meaningful relationships. Moreover, it fosters a spirit of giving, enabling us to contribute positively to society. Unfortunately, in today's materialistic world, many feel trapped in a relentless rat race, as our education system emphasizes hard skills. However, employers are increasingly valuing soft skills as well."

"Soft skills? What are those?" I asked curiously.

"Soft skills are the non-technical abilities that shape how we work and interact with others. They encompass effective communication, problem-solving, time management, empathy, and other essential traits. Being aware of our feelings and emotions is crucial for personal and professional development."

"How can I become more self-aware?" I pondered aloud.

"Great question! You can enhance your self-awareness through practices such as self-reflection, meditation, yoga, or simply spending quiet time alone. Remember how Naanu would sometimes observe 'Maun Vrata'? These practices help you connect with yourself, clarify what you truly want, and discern what feels right or wrong for you."

"What is 'Maun Vrata'?" I asked, trying to refresh my memory.

"Oh, you've forgotten?" she replied with a gentle smile. "Maun Vrata means 'vow of silence'. 'Maun' stands for silence, and 'Vrata' means a vow or a spiritual discipline. So when *Naanu* observes Maun Vrata, he commits to a period of silence, usually for spiritual growth, self-discipline, or inner reflection. It's something he practices as a form of meditation or mindfulness. In fact, it's also considered an act of devotion in several religions such as Hindu, Jain, and Buddhist traditions."

"I get it, Maa. Just like physical fitness is a key part of my daily routine, I need to add these mental exercises as well."

"Exactly! The first step toward self-awareness is prioritizing your health, including your diet. Nourishing your body with a balanced diet and engaging in regular exercise creates a synergy that enhances both your physical and mental potential, leading to lasting well-being and happiness.

Are you holding back your growth, Aadi?" she asked, looking intently at me.

"Hmm, I guess I never thought about it that way."

"By nature, we are meant to grow both physically and mentally. However, some people unknowingly hinder their own development. While we possess everything needed to thrive, temptations—such as the allure of processed foods—can lead us astray. We often trade our good health for unhealthy choices, ultimately falling victim to diseases. This reality is indeed disheartening."

I nodded, absorbing her words. "What about mental growth?"

"That's a great point! Take newborn babies, for example. They are spontaneous and expressive, reacting to stimuli with cries or giggles without hesitation. However, as we grow, we often become overly conscious of others' opinions. Questions like **'What will people say about me?'** can create barriers that hinder our mental growth, leading to fear, inhibitions, underperformance, frustration, disappointment, and ultimately, failure. While social awareness is important, we shouldn't let judgment affect us as long as we're not doing anything wrong. Do you agree?"

"Yes, Maa. I understand what you mean. This conversation feels quite therapeutic, and I'm ready to take charge of my life. I want to learn more from you." I had so many questions swirling in my mind.

"I now realize that I need to be mentally strong enough to not let disappointments and challenges hinder my growth. To cultivate self-awareness, I must fully understand my strengths and weaknesses. I remember attending a self-awareness workshop in college, and it was an exciting experience!"

"Sounds promising! But what did you find challenging?" she asked.

"Well, it was a bit scary. The more I tried to confront my weaknesses, the more fear took hold of me."

"So, what's holding you back from achieving your goals? Is it fear?" she asked, her tone curious. "Yes, I suppose that's it. Fear, definitely," I admitted, my voice barely above a whisper.

Fear is a prison we build for ourselves; to escape, we must first recognize that the key is in our hands.

Dear Readers,

Try this Pomodoro Dance Break.

Before diving into reading further, engage in a quick burst of movement to energize your brain and body. This will improve blood flow and enhance focus when you start reading.

How to do it:

Set a timer for 2-3 minutes.

Put on your favorite upbeat song.

Dance around as wildly or as rhythmically as you like!

After the song ends, sit down and start reading.

Scientific Basis: Physical movement releases endorphins, improves cognitive function, and boosts brain power. Dance breaks, in particular, improve mood and concentration.

Fun Element: You can add a theme to your dance break, such as dancing like an animal or pretending you're at a party in space!

10

FEAR

A Friend in Disguise

Maa shared with me a very interesting memory from her college days.

"It was my first Music Night at college and I was standing backstage, shuffling my feet nervously, my heart pounding, nervous about the crowd waiting for me. As my name was called out, I walked onto the stage, barely able to see the audience under the bright lights. I closed my eyes, took a deep breath, and let go of worrying about how it would turn out. I just focused on performing. That day, I learned something crucial: fear can either keep us trapped, or it can push us forward. The key is how we choose to face it.

The most successful people still experience fear; they've just learned how to manage it. They accept it, learn from it, and even use it as motivation. Think about the best public speakers, the ones who seem so confident, or public figures you admire. It's not that they're fearless. They've simply developed ways to turn fear into fuel.

One of the first steps is ***accepting your fears***. Your fears reveal areas where you can grow. Acknowledge them; they're not obstacles but tools for self-discovery. Avoiding your fears is like driving blindfolded; it only leads to trouble. By understanding what causes your fears, you gain insight into yourself, and that's a huge step forward.

But remember, don't procrastinate! Once you see your fears for what they are, many will seem like illusions or assumptions. Face these head-on and start solving any fears that still hold power over you. Getting guidance or support is okay; it's smart to seek advice from people who've walked a similar path.

On this journey, stay resilient. There will be setbacks, but every stumble is a chance to learn and come back stronger. Keep your vision in mind. Know that it's your life to build, and the mistakes you make are part of that process. People forget struggles when they see success like a tree that's ignored in winters but admired in bloom.

Lastly, keep checking in with yourself. Be your own critic before seeking feedback from others. Compare what you planned to do with the steps you've actually taken; the results will show how far you've come."

"Does that make sense?" Maa asked.

"Yes, I do get it. I must become aware of my fears, uncover their roots, get help, and stay focused through challenges," I replied, gradually recognizing the truth in her words.

Reflective Question:

What specific fears are currently holding you back from pursuing your goals?

Action Steps:

- **Find Your Fears:**

  Identify and write down the one most dominant fear that prevents you from achieving your goals. How has it impacted your decisions and actions?

- **Analyze Your Fear:**

  - **Ask Yourself:**

    If I confront this fear, what could be the worst-case scenario?

    Is this fear based on reality or merely on my assumptions?

  - **Seek Support:**

    Identify at least one mentor, friend, or coach who can help you navigate your fear.

  - **Plan of Action:**

    Start by tackling this one dominant fear first. Outline a step-by-step plan to confront this fear, including small, manageable actions that will lead you toward facing it head-on.

- **Practice Mindfulness:**

  Incorporate mindfulness techniques, such as deep breathing or meditation, into your daily routine.

- **Set Goals to Work on Your Fear:**

  Establish a short-term goal related to overcoming your fear. Celebrate even the smallest progress once you achieve it.

- **Reflect Regularly:**

  For the next few weeks, regularly assess your progress in confronting this fear. Reflect on what worked, what didn't, and how to improve.

- **Reframe Your Mindset:**

  Practice reframing negative self-talk about your fears into positive affirmations. For example, change "I am afraid of failing" to "Every challenge I face is an opportunity to learn and grow."

11

IS HAPPINESS PART OF YOUR DNA

Discovering Your Happiness Blueprint!

"**L**et me ask you another question! Aadi, are you naturally happy?" "What's naturally happy? I don't get it!" I replied. "Imagine, one day you fall sick with viral fever just before your final exams! You're stuck in bed battling fever while your friends are ready to ace the exams. What do you feel…? Feel grateful! Thank God that it wasn't dengue or the deadly COVID-19 virus. Be grateful for the people you've got to help you, the hands that feed you, take care of you, the medicines you have, the breath you can take!

Hope is the only thing stronger than fear!

This powerful line, penned down in the book Hunger Games, speaks volumes about tackling any challenge that comes our way. People have recovered from the deadliest diseases, survived the unsurvivable, and climbed the ladders of success from the depths of the gutter, only because they had hope.

Happiness isn't something you chase; it's something you cultivate within yourself, just like a skill or a habit, and maintaining happiness is an ongoing journey, not a one-time achievement. By cultivating gratitude, practicing mindfulness, contentment, and acceptance, nurturing relationships, and setting meaningful goals, we create a strong foundation for lasting happiness. You need to make happiness an integral part of who you are, like it's encoded in your DNA, and build a foundation for a life of joy and resilience," she said.

As I sat in the quiet of my room, reflecting on my journey, I found myself drawn to the four pillars that have shaped my understanding of happiness and fulfillment: gratitude, acceptance, productivity, and giving. Each of these elements interweaves with the others, creating a tapestry that not only supports me but also empowers those around me.

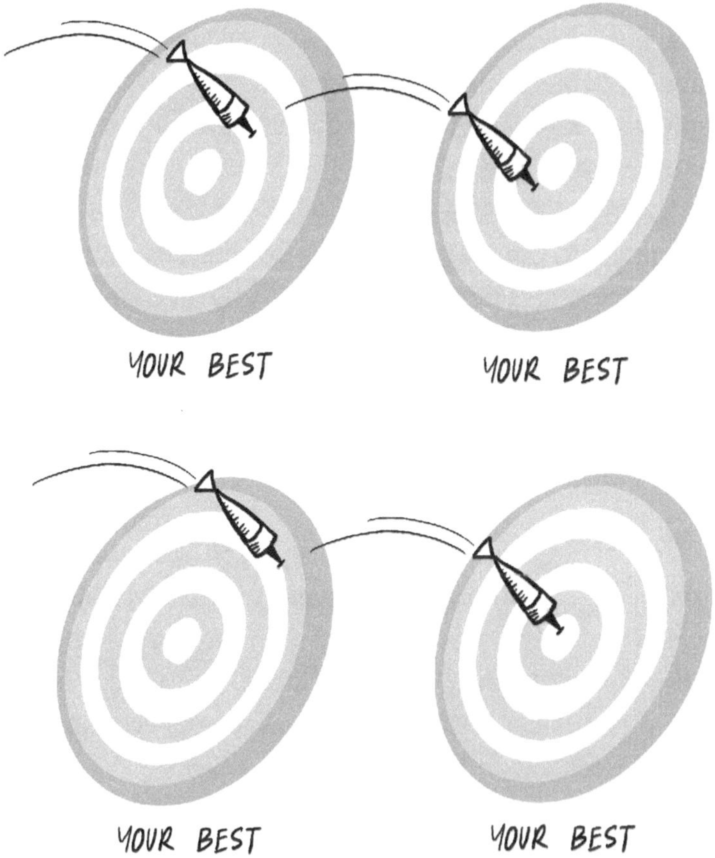

YOUR BEST   YOUR BEST

YOUR BEST   YOUR BEST

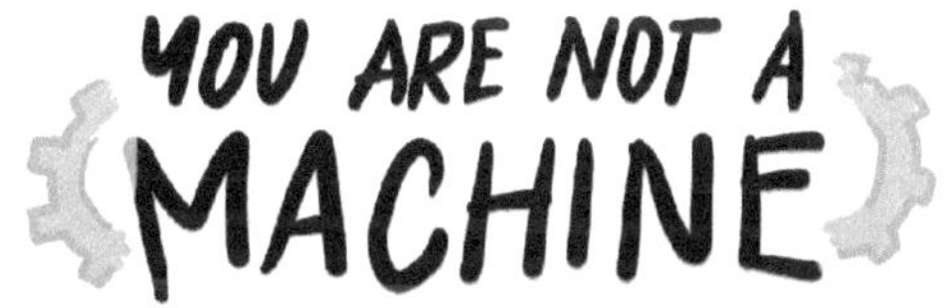

YOU ARE NOT A MACHINE

Your BEST will look different each day
(and that's totally okay!)

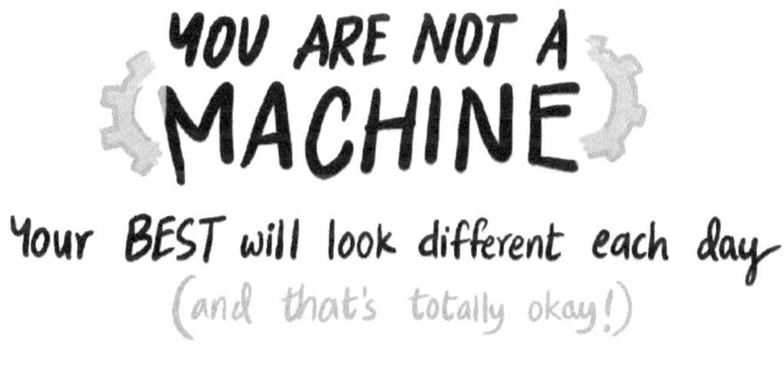

Gratitude was the first lesson I learned. I remember the days when I felt overwhelmed by the pressures of life, job searches, expectations, and uncertainties swirling around me like a storm. In those moments, I often forgot to appreciate the simple joys, the warmth of the sun on my face, the laughter shared with friends, and the support of my family. One day, my mother encouraged me to start a gratitude journal. "Aadi," she said, "when you write down what you're thankful for, you begin to see the beauty in everyday moments."

Taking her advice to heart, I started to jot down even the smallest things: a kind word from a stranger, a delicious meal, or simply a peaceful evening. With each entry, I noticed a shift in my perspective. Gratitude opened my eyes to the positive aspects of my life, even amid challenges. It became a powerful reminder that happiness often lies in the ordinary, waiting to be acknowledged.

As I delved deeper into my journey, I encountered *acceptance*. Accepting my circumstances, my limitations, and even my failures became crucial for my emotional well-being. It was difficult at first; I often grappled with feelings of inadequacy and self-doubt. However, I learned that acceptance didn't mean resignation. It was about recognizing where I stood and embracing it without the burden of *'what ifs'*.

I discovered that when I accepted my flaws, I could transform them into strengths. I wasn't perfect, and that was okay. Instead of wallowing in self-pity, I found the courage to face my weaknesses, learn from them, and use them as stepping stones for growth. This realization was liberating, it allowed me to free myself from the shackles of unrealistic expectations and societal pressures.

Productivity and growth came next. While acceptance helped me find peace in my current state, it didn't mean I could sit idle. I understood that growth was essential for true fulfillment. My journey involved pushing boundaries, setting goals, and stepping out of my comfort zone. I often reminded myself of the phrase, "Grow through what you go through."

The more I focused on personal development—whether it was improving my skills, seeking new opportunities, or pursuing my passions—the more fulfilled I felt. It wasn't always easy; there were days when hard work felt draining. Yet, each small effort contributed to my growth, revealing layers of potential I hadn't recognized before.

Finally, I realized the profound impact of *giving*. There's something incredibly fulfilling about sharing, whether it's my time, knowledge, or kindness. I found that acts of generosity created a ripple effect, spreading positivity not only to others but also back to me. Volunteering, mentoring peers, or simply being there for a friend in need reinforced my connections with those around me.

Being a giver opened my heart to the struggles of others, allowing me to empathize deeply. It reminded me that everyone faces battles, often unseen. Each act of giving brought a sense of purpose to my life, reinforcing the idea that we rise by lifting others. However, I also learned the importance of balance; it was essential to recharge and take care of myself to continue giving effectively.

As I look back on this journey, I see how gratitude, acceptance, productivity, and giving are not just isolated concepts but interconnected elements that enrich my life. They form the foundation upon which I build my happiness, resilience, and purpose. Each pillar supports the others, creating a holistic approach to living that allows me to navigate life's challenges with grace and optimism.

In embracing these four pillars, I've come to understand that life is not just about finding happiness for myself; it's about cultivating an environment where happiness can flourish for everyone around me.

And in this interconnectedness, I've discovered the blueprint for my happiness!

Happiness isn't just a fleeting emotion; it's woven into the fabric of who you are. Unravel the threads, and you'll find your unique happiness blueprint.

Reflective Question:

"What are the small moments or activities in your daily life that genuinely bring you joy, and how often do you take the time to appreciate them?"

Action Step:

Set aside a few minutes each day for the next week to *jot down three things* that made you smile or brought you happiness, no matter how small. At the end of the week, reflect on these moments. Consider how you can incorporate more of these joyful activities into your routine moving forward.

This practice aligns with findings from positive psychology, which emphasize the benefits of gratitude and mindfulness in enhancing overall well-being.

12

MY GUIDING STARS

Guided by Love, Driven by Purpose

"**S**o Aadi, you know that I have taught at two wonderful universities, right? I might not have shared this with you, but the time I spent there, and the students I interacted with left a lasting impact on me. Each day that I spent with them—my vibrant, energetic and incredibly hard-working students—wasn't just a source of joy, but learning for me. Each lecture, each shared interaction left us both enlightened and energized. During my lectures, I would often start sharing what my students loved to call *'Pravachans'* – life lessons wrapped in humor," she said, beaming.

While I thought that the word *'Pravachan'* was slightly cheesy, I could imagine how fun, lighthearted and motivating something of this sort could be during a lecture. It was her way of weaving life lessons in a manner that could effortlessly resonate with her students, and both enlighten and entertain!

Nevertheless, I rolled my eyes and humorously said, "Oh no, I hate it when teachers shower unwanted *gyan*, Maa."

Maa laughed with me, her eyes twinkling. "Oh, already skeptical about my *pravachans*, huh?" she teased. "But remember, these little lectures—whether for my students or for you—come from a place of wanting to see you all grow. I share them because I wish someone had told me these things back when I was young and battling my own insecurities! Each bit of the *gyan* is just a gentle nudge for you to figure out what's applicable in your case. ***Every person is different. What works for me might not work for you.***"

She paused, smiling. "Think of them as reminders, take what helps, and leave the rest. Well, as I was saying, each class had over 150 young girls and boys; coming from diverse backgrounds, education levels, and having different personalities. They weren't just learners; they were my guiding stars."

"Wow, Maa! That sounds incredible. You must have really loved them!" I responded.

Her voice softened as she said, "Yes, immensely, yet, in the midst of all that brilliance and joy, I noticed a few students struggling, particularly with confidence. It was heartbreaking to see some of them, so bright and talented, holding themselves back because of self-doubt. A few were timid and hesitant, weighed down by their lack of belief in themselves. And it wasn't just specific to the university, I noticed the same pattern in several other places. Despite their potential, many young people seemed burdened by doubt, crippled by underconfidence; not knowing how to move forward. On the other hand, some were overconfident, filled with big dreams but without a vision or the efforts to back them up. They were aimless, chasing illusions of success without the necessary grit. Then, there were those exceptionally talented but underutilized youth, lost in the distractions of life, and extremely unproductive. I couldn't help but feel a deep sense of responsibility to guide them, and these little bits of wisdom made all the difference."

I knew what she meant. Maa had a way of talking that could shift your whole perspective in just a few sentences. She didn't lecture or preach; she shared her life experiences, and they stayed with you.

"Do you see where this is going, Aadi?" she continued. "We all have our challenges and weaknesses, but we also possess the power to overcome them."

Maa looked at me thoughtfully. "We often hear that education can change our lives, that degrees in engineering, science, commerce, or the arts will open the doors to success. But if that were the case, then tell me, Aadi, why do we still have so many young people who feel stuck in a loop of finding a job or getting out of it? Why are they slipping into disappointment and frustration?"

I nodded, and as I sat pondering over what she'd just said, Maa got up. "Come, Aadi, let me share three of my dearest *pravachans* with you over a cup of coffee."

As we headed toward the kitchen, I saw Dad sitting in his armchair, lost in his own thoughts. He looked strikingly different from his usual self. His fierce expressions had softened into grief, and it felt as if my struggles weighed more on him than on me. I realized that anger was his way of trying to deal with a situation where he felt so helpless. I'd have to talk to him later once I had a bit more courage. I looked back at Maa, only to find her gently smiling at me, as if she had already heard the unspoken apology I contained within myself.

Pravachan 1: Your Educational Degree Doesn't Define You

"First and foremost, Aadi, you must understand that your college degree does not define your life and journey, and it is most certainly not the only key to your success. I have seen so many people solely relying on their certifications to get them a job, promotion, or respect. But, in my opinion, that couldn't be further from the real picture. Your degree and institution might open a few doors, sure, and it might give you access to bright minds and several resources, but at the end of the day, it depends on you and how you make the best of what you have been served." Noticing that I was unconvinced, she shot a serious but not too serious look at me, demanding some attention, and continued, "There are thousands of people out there with fancy degrees, yet so many of them are still struggling. Why? Because they thought that their degree was enough. It's not. What matters more is your grit, your ability to learn, unlearn, and keep growing long after you've left the classroom," she said. "So, if you are burdened by the thought of not opting for the 'perceived' superior degree, or not getting admission to the college of your dreams, let's first start with getting rid of that self-imposed guilt. Believe me, this shift of perspective will make all the difference in the world."

"Your worth is not measured by a piece of paper; it's defined by your actions, values, and the impact you make in the world."

I couldn't help but admit to what she was saying. In the past, it felt easier to lie back on the regrets of not getting the golden ticket of a premium degree in a top-tier university. But there might be so many examples around us of people graduating from these very institutions, getting placed in the top companies, yet feeling stuck in their jobs; like square pegs being fit in round molds. On the other hand, there are business tycoons who haven't had any formal education but have redefined the course of their industry, simply because they hustled, adapted, and never stopped learning.

I realized that my degree alone wasn't going to make me successful, it was just a tool. In the hands of a craftsman, it could be used to sculpt a masterpiece; a masterpiece of my dreams, not someone else's. "Keep learning throughout your life, beyond your classroom, Aadi; remember, a painter uses an entire arsenal of brushes to bring life to a canvas, so you can't possibly expect just one to shape your entire life."

Pravachan 2: Fear of Failure Is Your Biggest Enemy

"Now Aadi if you have to embark upon a lifetime journey of learning, can you tell me what comes hand-in-hand with that?" Maa asked. "Well, one of my main fears of learning new skills is the thought of being so miserably bad at them that I just don't feel like trying," I helplessly admitted.

"Exactly, Aadi! You're absolutely correct AND wrong at the same time, wonderful! Now let me explain this: Failure is inevitable; you can't possibly be headed in a direction without falling and failing. And fear; it is ingrained in our DNA, and we can't function without it. The most interesting thing is that both fear and failure are essential for your success, but the fear of failure is your biggest enemy. That's what really holds you back."

At first, I didn't fully understand what she meant, so she explained, "Failure is feedback. It's the universe's way of showing you what didn't work, so you can try again, afresh, or maybe try something else. But fear… fear is what stops you from even trying in the first place."

She continued with certainty, "When you were young, you'd ask an endless series of questions about anything and everything that caught your eye. I still remember the time you started walking. It was after falling so many times, in the most brutal ways, but you made it, didn't you? Why? Because you didn't just sit and start questioning your abilities, fearing judgment and ridicule. Every time you fell, you either cried or laughed it off and tried again."

I began to understand where she was going with this. "I think I get it, Maa. There have been countless occasions when I hesitated to speak up in meetings or pass on the opportunity to lead big projects just because I have this innate fear of performing terribly, and by doing so, I feel stuck in my current position while my colleagues get recognized and promoted.

I need to start taking small leaps of faith, allow myself to make mistakes, and most importantly, learn from them."

She told me how some of her students who were too scared to apply for internships or jobs at a big firm thought they were not good enough. Or would avoid speaking up in class and asking questions, worried they'd say something stupid. But the thing was, every time they pushed through that fear—whether it was spontaneous speaking in front of a huge audience or applying for a role they didn't think they'd ever get—it wasn't as bad as they imagined.

Maa's words were right: failure didn't hurt nearly as much as the regret of not trying. And she made sure I knew that facing my fear would look different than how others faced theirs, it was about making *my* own peace with failure because at the end of the day, I could never fail in my eyes if I got back up and tried again.

Pravachan 3: Success is a Process, Not a Destination

Maa sat there, weaving all the threads of my life like a magician, as she asked me, "Aadi, at what point in your life would you call yourself successful?" For a second, I was stumped by the question, mostly because I didn't have a unique answer, so I just went ahead with the conventional one in my head, "Maa, I think I'll be successful when I am placed in a high position, with a heavy income coming every month, and I don't like to admit this, but when people think of me in high regard; almost in awe. That is when I'll call myself successful…" I trailed off the last few words, seeing Maa's lips pursed in disagreement while her eyes conveyed a sense of patience and calm, almost expecting this answer as she said, "Success isn't a destination, Aadi. It's not a place you arrive at, and then you're done. *It's a process.* It's not about where you end up, but more about who you become along the way."

Maa gave me an example of one of her colleagues—on the surface, he was the shining picture of success— a wealthy owner of a beautiful home, luxurious cars, and everything that a person dreams of acquiring. However, despite all his achievements, he remained unhappy. He spent his entire life chasing the next milestone, always thinking that the next accomplishment, or another treasure, would finally bring him the success he so desperately craved. Yet, each new success left him feeling just as unfulfilled. Ma explained that while all these milestones can give us a sense of success, they were in fact only a series of external goals. In reality, true success is about appreciating the journey, the lessons, growth, and resilience gained along the way. It's about who you become through the struggles, not just what you achieve. In the end, you should be able to look back at the fleeting years of your life and cherish everything; the good, the bad and the ugly.

The idea was so far from what I imagined. To me, it had always been about the unattainable titles that were out of my reach – a job title, salary, recognition; everything else in the way was either a setback or my incapabilities. Why did I never think about appreciating where I am in the present, and how far I have come along?

She continued with a cautious tone, "Aadi, life is far too complex to be measured by accolades and external praises. If you're only focused on the finish line, you might miss out on the entire race. For all you know, there were some beautiful stops along the way."

Success is not a final destination; it's a journey of growth, learning, and resilience that shapes who you become along the way

Maa's three beautiful pearls of wisdom struck a deep chord within me. It felt like a fresh, cool breeze soothing my burning soul from within. These weren't just random lessons sprung out to pass the time in a lecture, nor were they an endless list of complex tasks that no one could even fathom completing. They were so simple, so natural... things I almost felt I'd known all along. Yet, they held such profound importance that I was certain, if followed, they would change the course of my life.

13

TAKE THE FIRST STEP

Your Journey Starts Here!

By now, I had begun to grasp the strength of a resilient mind. To tackle my chaotic career and life, I turned to Maa and asked, "I appreciate what we've discussed so far, Maa, but at the end of the day, I need to begin by understanding what I should do to create a fulfilling life and career. Where do I start?"

"**INITIATIVE**," she said, pausing to gauge my reaction, and I couldn't help but wonder, was the answer to my complex question really as simple as a single word?

She continued, "Initiative is the most powerful tool that can shape or rebuild our lives, careers, habits, relationships, and personalities. It reveals your hidden potential and brings out the leader within you. I believe it's the first step toward real progress. If you don't take action at the right time, pushing past your fears, assumptions, and doubts, you risk losing the opportunities meant for you. Nothing we've discussed today would have been possible if I hadn't taken the initiative to start this conversation, and if you hadn't seized the chance to open up about your feelings and emotions. Got it? Initiative reflects self-drive, awareness, insight, and motivation. The more you practice it, the easier it becomes."

"So, should I directly send my resume to companies, instead of relying on my contacts to give me referrals or waiting for that perfect opportunity to come knocking at my door?" I could feel a subtle shift in my mindset.

"Why not, Aadi? Take the first step by applying to companies without hesitation, and learn from each interview; even if they lead to rejections. But you know, it's more than just job applications. Initiative is about cultivating a habit that enriches your life. When you see someone in need, offer help. Reflect on where you might be going wrong and decide to make a change. Don't wait for others to guide you; take action. If something is broken, fix it. Speak up about issues that need addressing, identify opportunities, and seize them. Go the extra mile at home and work. This will not only help you build strong and lasting connections with your colleagues and bosses, but will also add a quality to your personality that will be valued anywhere you go."

Taking initiative is the spark that ignites change; it's the courage to step forward when others hesitate.

She continued, "You asked me about how you should create a fulfilling career, right? Well, you need to *set your intention on your purpose* and take charge of your own trajectory because where better to take initiative than for your own life! How about we set a month's target to explore your career path? You must start by chalking a plan to attain tangible results, and I will be right there to guide you. Do you think you're ready for the challenge?"

I nodded excitedly, trying to drown the negative thoughts that threatened to demotivate me before I could start, and focused on the steps I needed to take instead.

"Great! I know a month might sound too ambitious, but it's all about staying focused and committed. In a month, you can break your goals down, sharpen your skills, and even prepare yourself for interviews. It's not just about landing any job; it's about finding the right one that aligns with your values and aspirations. With the right plan and determination, you'll be amazed at how much progress you can make!"

Reflective Question:

"What's one area in your life where you've been waiting for things to change, and how can taking initiative help you create that change?"

Action Step:

Identify a situation in your life where you feel stuck or passive. This week, take one proactive step—such as setting a meeting, starting a new project, or initiating a conversation—to address it. Write down the outcome of your action and reflect on how taking that initiative made you feel and what changes it led to.

14

BRANDING YOUR GROWTH

Define Your Path. Own Your Journey!

"**A**adi, now that you are all set to embark upon this one-month journey of transforming your career, you should understand a concept that I like to call: *Branding Your Own Growth.*"

I wondered what this phrase could mean. Up until now, I had heard about branding company logos, products and even people. But branding one's own growth? It just seemed paradoxical. "What does that mean, Maa?" I inquired. She excitedly began, "So Aadi, I'm sure you already know that every company creates their own brand, something that they are known and valued for. Every successful brand, with all its features and benefits, has a unique individuality, and a unique personality. Similarly, branding your personal growth means consciously shaping the way you develop as a person, a professional, and a member of society. Aadi, it's more than just setting goals, it's about creating an intentional image of who you are and who you're becoming. Just like a company or product is known for certain qualities, you can build a personal identity based on your strengths, values, and the decisions you make."

Maa believed the key to 'Personal Branding' was *consistency and authenticity*, to which she added, "A major part of '*branding your growth*' is staying true to who you are. *Authenticity* plays a huge role in personal branding because people can sense when you're not being genuine," she further emphasized, "People don't just admire success; they admire the journey, the struggles, and the authenticity behind it. To be known for your growth, you have to embrace both your strengths and areas for improvement. By working on yourself consistently and aligning your actions with your values, you build a brand that resonates deeply with those around you."

When Maa explained this to me, I started reflecting on how I had been approaching life. I was chasing milestones, trying to measure up to expectations, without realizing that I was losing sight of what mattered most, who I wanted to be. That's when it hit me that *branding your growth* is about being deliberate with your actions, decisions, and the path you take. It's about asking, "What am I known for? What values do I represent? What legacy am I building?"

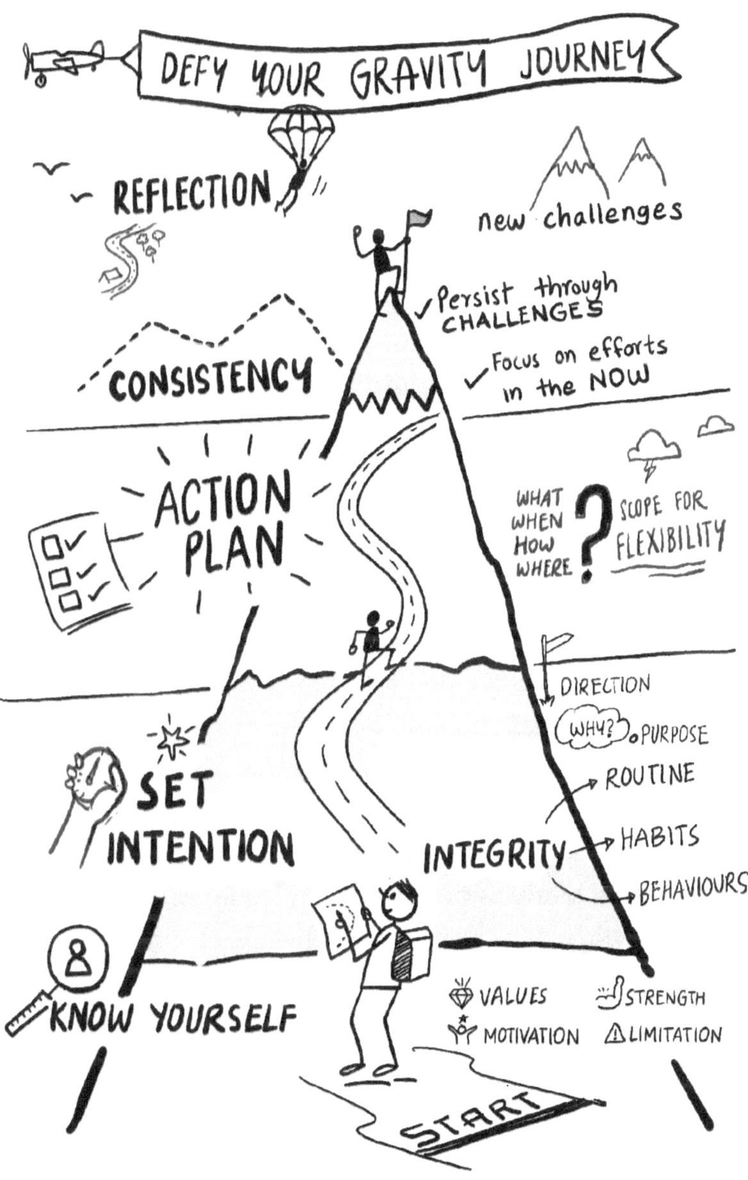

As Maa often said, *"The first step to branding your growth is taking initiative."* She reminded me that every time I took a step toward bettering myself, I was not just working on my goals, I was building my brand. The more I practiced taking initiative, the more natural it would become. It's easy to get stuck waiting for someone to guide you or tell you what to do, but Maa always said, "Don't wait. Take action, take charge." The small steps I took every day, like seeking out new skills or learning from my mistakes, were building the foundation of my personal brand.

One of the most powerful lessons I learned from Maa is *aligning my growth with purpose.* She cautioned me, "Aadi, personal growth without purpose can feel empty. Branding your growth isn't just about moving forward; it's about moving forward with direction. You need to be clear about '*why*' you're growing and what you're working toward. It's not just about success or financial stability, those things are fleeting. It's about shaping a life that reflects your values, inspires others, and adds meaning to your journey."

She always emphasized that having a clear sense of purpose keeps you grounded, even during challenges. "When you know *why* you're doing something," she said, "every step feels more meaningful. Whether it's a career move, a personal decision, or a relationship choice, when your actions align with your deeper purpose, you're not just achieving goals, but taking another step toward building a legacy."

I listened to her intently as she continued, *"Reinventing yourself is not a sign of instability*; it's a sign of resilience. Each time we grow, we're adding another layer to our brand, another dimension to who we are. When you make learning and reinvention part of your personal growth, you're telling the world that you're not static. You are committed to evolving." Mom further added, "Perhaps the most rewarding part of branding your own growth is the ripple effect it creates. When you stay true to your values and work on yourself with consistency and purpose, you **build trust with those around you**. People begin to see you as someone who is reliable, someone who is constantly striving to be better, and someone who inspires them to do the same." By now, I knew that Maa always believed that success was not just about what you achieve but also about the impact you have on others.

"When people see you taking charge of your life and growing with purpose," she said, "they're inspired to do the same." **And that's when it all clicked for me.** I realized that 'branding your growth' was not just about standing out for myself; it was about becoming someone who motivates and uplifts those around me. There are a lot of people who are successful in conventional and unconventional terms, but their journey would resonate with the masses when they show a dynamic, purpose-driven, authentic trajectory that strives to unite people, emotions and purposes together. The importance of this concept went way beyond my career and touched every aspect of my life – from my interactions with co-workers at the office, contributing to society, to the way I perceived myself.

"Your growth is your brand; define it with intention and authenticity, and watch it shape the world around you."

But somewhere during our conversation about 'branding your growth', a question came to my mind, "What values do you find most effective while branding your growth, Maa?"

She said, "That's a great question, Aadi! So, think of values as your personal compass, or, better yet, your trusty GPS. You wouldn't want to end up in the middle of nowhere just because you didn't check the directions, right?" she asked, winking. "They exist in our lives like the roots of a tree, holding us steady, no matter how fiercely the winds blow. To begin with, we must learn to listen to that tiny inner voice that constantly whispers, reminding us to do what is right, especially when taking the wrong turn is the most comfortable choice, that's **integrity**. Every time that we choose the right path, within and beyond the scope of an audience, we're building something priceless, **self-respect**. Integrity is the foundation of developing trust in yourself, which isn't just about avoiding mistakes but embracing honesty in every decision."

She continued, "Then comes **perseverance**. It is similar to an unbreakable thread of grit, determination and energy, urging us to keep going, especially when the journey feels like an uphill battle. Life will push you to your limits, and in those moments of discomfort, when you feel stretched and unsure, is when you're truly growing. Even the most treacherous trails feel easier to conquer when you are surrounded by positivity, and what better way to nurture that than by developing the habit of kindness? **Kindness** stems out of love for others. We must consider that we are all together on this journey of life and that whatever good we do to others will return back to us in one form or the other. It then becomes easier for us to appreciate others' struggles in life, being empathetic to their situation and celebrating their glory. The best part about practicing the art of kindness is that the person who most benefits from this is You! *You become kinder to yourself, and allow yourself to freely fail, learn and enjoy life in all its phases.*"

As I let this sink in, Maa suggested that I keep a journal of my experiences, which I thought was a brilliant idea. Writing would allow me to reflect on my journey and see how I was growing through these values and more.

Dear Readers,

Set Your Goals, Shape Your Future

It's time to take control of your journey. Use this simple goal-setting formula to make your dreams a reality:

1. **Define Your Goal:** What do you want to achieve? Be specific. (Example: I want to complete an online course on digital marketing.)

2. **Break it Down:** Divide your goal into smaller, manageable tasks. (Example: Week 1: Research courses, Week 2: Enroll, Week 3: Complete the first module.)

3. **Set a Deadline:** Assign a realistic timeline for each task. Deadlines help keep you accountable.

4. **Stay Flexible:** Life happens. Don't give up if things don't go as planned. Adjust your timeline but stay committed to the goal.

5. **Celebrate Milestones:** Every small victory deserves recognition. Reward yourself when you complete a step.

REWRITE YOUR STARS

Your Journey, Your Rules, Make It Happen!

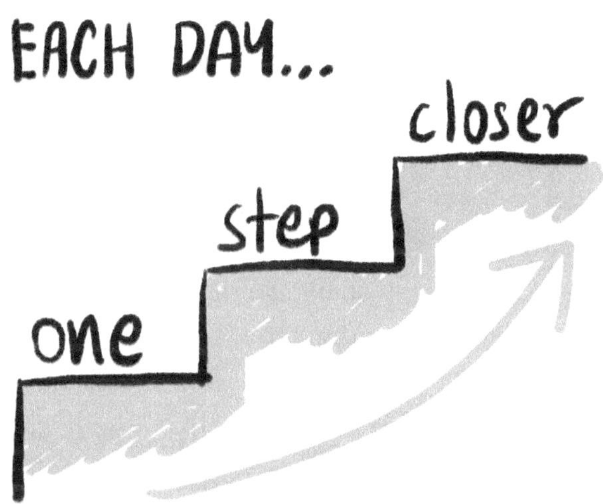

As the sun peeked over the horizon today, I felt a bubbling mix of excitement and those pesky nerves. It was like waking up to a blank canvas, just waiting for me to splash my dreams and goals all over it. Sure, I've had my fair share of struggles and doubts, but today felt different. I was ready to grab this day and make it mine, another chance to take charge of my life.

Through the long conversations full of self-reflection with Maa, I realized that I wasn't stuck in my life because of external circumstances alone. There was a narrative which I had accepted about my potential, one that quietly limited me, not realizing how deeply the expectations of the people around me influenced my opinion of myself. I was living by the rules and definitions others had set for me, unwritten 'rules' about what I could achieve, what success should look like, and what a career path ought to be.

Maa encouraged me to shed these beliefs, reframe my situation, and challenge those internal limits that were holding me back. By doing so, I will not only transform my personality but also: ***"Rewrite my stars."***

Would it be an overnight transformation? No. Would it be easy? Not at all. Will I have to massively challenge the way people make me feel? Absolutely. But through the entire process, I will liberate myself and allow myself to soar high like a bird, fall like a hatchling, and rebuild like an eagle that almost plucks itself to death so that it can flourish for decades.

You are the author of your own story;
embrace your unique journey and write the
rules that guide you toward your dreams

So I made a pact with myself: I would rewrite my journey by focusing on what I could do every day to defy the limits I'd unconsciously placed on myself. Instead of passively waiting for a big break, I'd create small, meaningful steps to get closer to the person I wanted to become.

This new approach didn't mean that I had it all figured out or that I'd have a clear path ahead. But every time I felt lost, I reminded myself that I had the power to keep moving forward, to ***defy my gravity***. Each day would be a chance to live by my own rules, not the ones others had set for me. I had the tools, the values, and the drive to reshape my journey. It was time to rewrite my stars.

Now that I had decided to rewrite my stars, I knew the road ahead was not going to be easy. I also knew I would encounter many barriers to maintaining my resolve. So I set out to identify the probable roadblocks on the way. I listed these in descending order, starting with the most probable to the least, or those rare occasional encounters in my case. Based on this, I wanted to figure out what my next steps should be.

Likely Roadblocks Ahead:

1. Looking for perfection
2. Discipline
3. Lack of knowledge
4. Laziness
5. Self-doubt
6. Being unorganized
7. No structured routine
8. Personal health
9. Lack of focus
10. Unable to multitask
11. Lack of knowledge

12. Lack of motivation
13. Unable to mobilize resources/help/support
14. Consistency in efforts
15. Lack of functional skills
16. Lack of physical activity

Envisioning these roadblocks gave me the power to make plans for addressing them before they can transform into the barriers threatening to keep me imprisoned.

Among this list of roadblocks, my worst enemy was *'looking for perfection'*, or waiting for the perfect moment to come knocking at my doorstep. Most of the time, this has been the reason why I kept procrastinating and delaying things in my life. For example, while striving to draft the perfect pitch, I ended up never talking to my boss about my dream project. Had I acknowledged that things don't become perfect on the first try, rather requiring continuous efforts, thoughts, and brainstorming from a variety of people, I would have started by taking the leap of faith and embracing imperfection.

I remembered Maa had once told me perfection is a tricky thing. It's like chasing a mirage – you see it, but the closer you get, the farther away it seems. According to her, if one kept waiting for the 'perfect' moment, the chances of missing out on all the opportunities would certainly be higher. She'd once told me, "Aadi, sometimes, it's better to start messy and figure things out as you go. Action creates momentum, and before you know it, you'll be further along than you ever imagined. Don't let perfection cripple you – just take the first step, and the rest will follow."

The next challenge I often faced was being *'disciplined'*, to which Maa explained, "Discipline is all about doing what you don't feel like doing, knowing it's good for you. For instance, you've decided to wake up at 5 a.m. every day to start fresh. But how will you do this if you continue to live like a night owl? That's where discipline comes in. It's about sticking to that routine consistently and eliminating any distractions along the way.

Now, we all do know this to some extent, but how do you build such discipline? You must start by modifying small habits, set realistic goals which you can accomplish every day, and the rest is like a chain reaction, these regular actions will become habits, and you will continue building your muscle of discipline."

Building self-discipline is key to achieving personal goals, maintaining focus, and staying on track. Here are some practical tips to strengthen self-discipline:

1. **Set Clear, Specific Goals**

   Define exactly what you want to achieve. Vague goals lead to vague efforts—clarity is the key. Break down the big stuff into small, bite-sized tasks so you can see your progress.

2. **Develop a Routine**

   Consistency is crucial for self-discipline and really makes a difference. Create a daily routine that aligns with your priorities and stick to it. A structured day reduces decision fatigue and keeps you on track.

3. **Start Small**

   Don't overwhelm yourself. Start with small, doable tasks and build from there. Knocking out these little wins builds confidence, prepares you, and gives you the momentum to take on bigger challenges.

4. **Remove Temptations**

   Find out what's diverting your focus (like social media or binge-watching shows) and minimize them. Setting yourself up in an environment free from temptation will make it easier to stay disciplined.

5. **Time Management Tricks**

   Set specific time blocks for tasks using techniques like the Pomodoro method (25 minutes work, 5-minute break). This improves focus and prevents burnout.

6. **Stay Accountable**

   Track your progress and hold yourself accountable. Whether through journaling, habit trackers, or sharing your goals with someone you trust, accountability encourages discipline.

7. **Reward Yourself**

   Celebrate little wins! Whether it's a break or a treat, giving yourself something to look forward to after a task makes the hard work more fun.

   This motivates you to stay disciplined.

8. **Develop a strong "Why"**

   Know why you're going after your goals. A strong reason will keep you going, even when the excitement wears off.

9. **Learn to Say No**

   Sometimes you have to say "no" to distractions or things that don't serve your goals. Prioritize what matters most and don't overcommit.

10. **Embrace Failure as Feedback**

    Mistakes happen. Don't get discouraged—think of failures as lessons, as opportunities to learn and improve. Self-discipline is a journey, and setbacks are part of the process.

11. **Stay Mindful**

    Mindfulness keeps you in control of your choices. When you're aware of your impulses, you can make better decisions that align with your goals.

12. **Visualize Success**

    Picture what it'll feel like when you hit your goals. That mental image will keep you motivated and help you stay disciplined.

By incorporating these tips, you'll gradually build a strong foundation of self-discipline, which will help you achieve your personal and professional goals.

The third roadblock I felt was *'lack of knowledge'*. I asked Maa, "All this is definitely relevant, but I think one of the most constant challenges I face is my lack of knowledge; especially related to the industry I am working in. It isn't a mindset I can change; what I don't know, I don't know… and it's so hard to move forward in the world with confidence when you lack the essential skills! It fills me with self-doubt and helplessness."

She nodded understandingly and said, "I know that navigating the complexities of knowledge can be daunting, Aadi. Learning is an essential part of personal and professional growth as it opens doors to new opportunities and broadens our understanding of the world. Moreover, with the vast amount of information coming from every possible direction, it can be quite overwhelming. It's completely normal to feel uncertain at times, especially when you're striving to grasp new concepts. But you must embrace a *growth mindset* that can help turn those feelings of self-doubt into opportunities for growth and discovery. Say, someone asks you whether you know about a recent technology, why can't you simply say, 'I don't know it… yet'. There is no harm in acknowledging to others that you're unaware of things; in fact, some of the greatest intellectuals are often the ones who continuously and unapologetically admit to not knowing things so that they can learn it at that very instance!"

It was hard for me to see myself doing this, but I could see the importance of overcoming this fear. There was no hiding the fact that I had to learn a lot of things; I knew it, my colleagues knew it, and so did my bosses, so why should I not seek help? I had to accept my current level of expertise, and then, simply start working on honing the skills without overthinking about the perfection with which I am learning. Understanding this was like a huge weight being lifted off my shoulders, and it allowed me to critically analyze the root cause of each roadblock with compassion and determination.

TIPS TO ST
SELF-DIS
SET
CLEAR SPECIFIC
GOALS
DEVELOP
ROUTIN
STAY
ACCOUNTABLE
YUM!
REWARD
YOURSELF
DEVELOP A
STRONG
'WHY'
STOP
LEARN TO
SAY
'NO'

THEN
LINE

START
SMALL

TIME
NAGEMENT
TRILKS

REMOVE
TEMPTATIONS

ISUALIZE
JCCESS

STAY
MINDFUL

EMBRACE
FAILURE AS
FEEDBACK

16

THE QUIET STRENGTH OF CHOOSING

In Every Choice Lies the Seed of Transformation

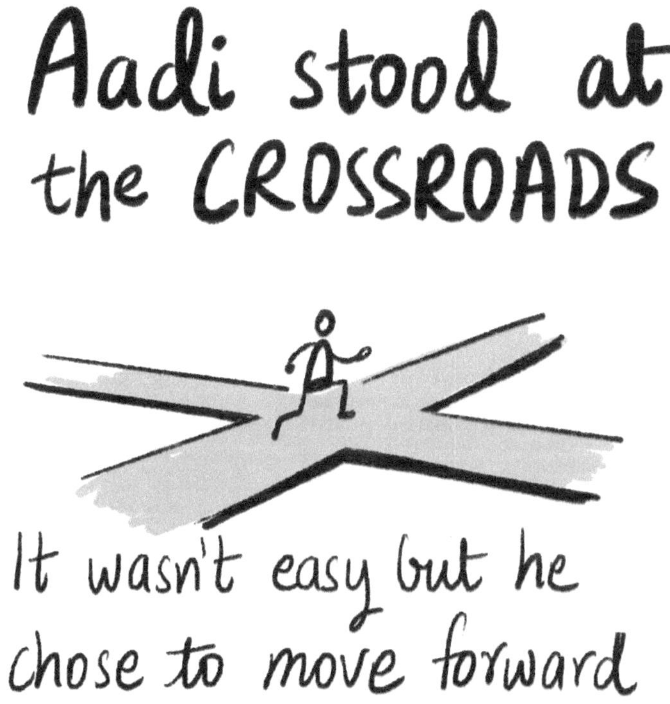

Reflecting on my journey, I realize that each challenge, each setback, and each conversation with my mom had led me to something much deeper than just finding a job. The path I was on was about finally taking control of my life and understanding what it meant to choose rather than drift. I had spent so long paralyzed by the fear of making the wrong move, as if one mistake would send me spiraling backward. But the reality was that the real decision lay in who I wanted to become, regardless of any individual outcome.

After weeks of gradual changes, I felt a difference. Slowly but surely, I was learning to trust my instincts, setting boundaries, and holding myself accountable in a way I never had before. Each morning brought its share of doubts, but I noticed that I wasn't running from it anymore. My mom's words echoed in my head, challenging me to not just think, but act. And, surprisingly, I found myself taking the plunge, over and over again, making small decisions that felt big to me.

I started by tenderly reaching out to my father and speaking with him. Sometimes adults can be as bad with words as children, so there is no harm in falling back on the most natural form of expression: crying. I spent the entire evening speaking with him, shedding a few tears and making him understand my point of view and my struggles; something we had never discussed before. He reciprocated by sharing his thoughts and darkest fears, and explaining what made him act so harshly with me. Somewhere along the tearful eyes and tired lines on his face, I saw the love he had for me.

In terms of habits, I'd begun embracing simple, consistent routines. I started waking up earlier, sticking to a daily list, and setting goals that I broke down into manageable steps. There was a quiet pride in knowing I was capable of following through. The truth was, it felt satisfying to set a goal and achieve it, even the small ones. They added up, giving me a sense of momentum I hadn't felt in a long time. I was no longer living in response to the pressures around me; I was creating a rhythm of my own. It was grounding.

Networking became an essential part of my journey. I discovered the power of community by surrounding myself with like-minded individuals who shared their experiences, wisdom, and support. Attending events and connecting with mentors opened new doors for me. Each conversation felt like a brick being laid in the foundation of my future.

Then came the two job offers, almost like an exam after all these months of self-discovery. In my hands, I held both possibilities, each one representing a step forward, yet I couldn't help but feel that familiar hesitation, the fear of making the 'wrong' choice. My first instinct was to freeze, to sit in that place of indecision indefinitely. But this time was different. I wasn't the same person who'd been so lost a few months ago.

I remembered what my mom had said about action, about how the only way to know the next step was to take it. I had come to learn that no amount of planning or strategizing could replace the clarity that action would give me. So, I looked at those two offers, not as a choice between perfect options, but as a decision about the direction I wanted to move toward. I wasn't seeking certainty; I was seeking growth. So, steadying my breath, I chose one of the offers. I knew very well that the journey didn't end by getting the job; in fact, it was just the beginning. I had been here before, at the brink of change and surrounded by opportunities, and I had failed; failed miserably. Even though my past mistakes and downfalls haunted me, I was aware of what I needed to do differently in order to overcome my demons, one step at a time. And if I did fail, I knew now that I would not stop.

While the footsteps I leave behind me may be
frail, covered by snow.

Even though I wanted to stop, maybe the
world wanted that too,

You should know that I ran, walked, limped
and crawled

I did everything I could before I disappeared
from the path itself because now I flew.

17

TRANSFORMING YOUR TRANSFORMATION

The Journey Beyond Growth Begins Here

By now, you must be kind of sick of me, no? You must be hoping to have had a beautiful ending in the last chapter. Aadi finally overcame his fears, dismissed his doubts about the perfect job, and started working toward his growth within and beyond his career. The End!

Not quite yet. I nervously tapped my foot as I sat at my desk, minutes before a huge presentation where I not only had to host but also give a thorough briefing of our current project to a panel of customers. Saying that I was terrified would be an understatement. I'd never given a speech longer than five minutes; that too was when I was surrounded by the familiar faces of my classmates in college. This was a different ball game altogether. What made matters worse was the fact that the previous month leading up to this presentation was nothing short of a disaster. I messed up every possible thing; missed deadlines, made silly mistakes, stuttered while asking questions, gave some mediocre ideas, all of which just made me more tense and falter again. Things weren't supposed to be this way, after I had worked like a madman, spent nights doing work, researching and preparing for every assignment, learning the technical and soft skills that were required. I even journaled, networked, and asked questions. Maa had told me that things would get better, and to some extent they had, but I was still ultimately failing, wasn't I? For a moment, I felt like that boy who couldn't escape the shadows of his past. I was afraid of being labeled as a failure again, even after having done everything right.

I closed my eyes; just as these thoughts threatened to swallow my newfound determination to escape this recurring pattern of failure, and the growth I made over the last few months seemed to be crumbling, I remembered three words: ***Defy Your Gravity.*** Defying your gravity and transforming your transformation and growth, as I'm learning, never stops; it has to keep evolving. Just because we reach a milestone doesn't mean we stop pushing ourselves. We transform by facing setbacks, observing where we need to improve, and finding our way through.

I took a deep breath as my boss called out my name. It was my time to speak, and I found myself walking toward the podium. I shed all the layers of my past as if they were nothing more than a change of clothes and timidly smiled at the audience, eagerly waiting for me to speak. This time, I saw them differently. I didn't think of them as a group of hyenas just waiting to pounce on me for making a mistake. Neither were they a group of distracted teenagers just waiting for me to finish. I saw each and every one of them as a learning opportunity; they all had something to teach me, be it patience, technical skills, courage, experience, or simply a smile. By stopping to think about them, I could focus on who I was, what I wanted to say, how to convey my thoughts, what I am passionate about, what I want to get out of this speech for myself, and what I have to offer to the masses.

It was far from perfect, but I did it. While the claps were subtle, I knew that there was someone cheering at me from within for conquering my fears and not letting them define how I presented myself to the world. It was the one person who mattered the most: me.

If you're on a similar journey of self-improvement, know that the growth that got you this far is just the beginning. It's tempting to think we're done once we reach a goal, but it's a lifelong practice. I've learned to regularly check in with myself, like my mom calls it, practicing 'Nirakh Parakh' self-introspection, to make sure I'm still on track. This isn't about judging myself harshly but making sure I'm staying true to the values I believe in.

In times when projects fail or situations feel messy, that's when I remind myself that growth isn't always a straight shot to success. Sometimes, it feels more like playing a song for the first time, where you keep missing notes until, eventually, you get it right. Each stumble is a chance to improve, so I stumble and I fall, never stopping, and adorning a smile all the while.

Some of the most powerful takeaways I've found in this journey of *Defy Your Gravity* are:

1. **Hold Tight to Your Dreams:** Set an intention with a clear purpose in mind.

   Challenges will come, and dreams may seem far off. But each action you take, each skill you develop, is getting you closer to them. Don't let temporary setbacks make you give up on what you truly want.

2. **Consistency Creates Transformation:** Make a plan and follow it through. Small, daily actions have the power to shape your future. When things get hard, just keep moving, no matter how slow the pace may seem.

3. **Anchor Yourself in Values:** Honesty, Authenticity, integrity, kindness, these aren't just words; they're the roots that ground you in every situation. Living by these values makes the journey meaningful and worth every effort.

4. **Focus on the Journey, Not Just the Destination:** Enjoy the process, be kind to yourself, and remember that growth is ongoing. There's no 'end' point; the journey itself is where we find fulfillment.

5. **Self-Reflection Matters:** Practicing regular self-reflection keeps you on track. It's not about criticizing yourself but observing where you can grow. Sometimes, stepping back and recalibrating is all you need to stay true to who you're becoming.

This journey of growth is about defying limitations, transforming every setback into a stepping stone, and creating a life of purpose. So if you're reading this, wondering when things will finally fall into place, remember that the real magic is in the journey itself. Every step forward, every failure overcome, is part of a transformation that's never truly finished. Keep moving and keep defying your gravity, because the best version of yourself is still out there, waiting to be realized.

As I stand here now, I can feel those *euphoric rays* of newfound confidence and clarity washing over me, illuminating my path ahead. The term 'Euphoric Rays' perfectly encapsulates this feeling, those moments of pure joy and relief that come when you finally embrace who you are and let go of what holds you back – when you truly *Defy Your Gravity – Rise Above Your Challenges And Embrace Your Potential.*

CONSISTENCY creates TRANSFORMATION

SELF-REFLECTION MATTERS

HOLD TIGHT TO YOUR DREAMS

FOCUS ON THE JOURNEY, NOT JUST THE DESTINATION

ANCHOR YOURSELVES IN VALUES

DIG DEEP

CHALLENGE YOUR INNER CRITIC

TAKE TINY STEPS

REACH OUT

CHECK YOURSELF

CELEBRATE the LITTLE WINS

Reflection Question:

What fears or beliefs have been keeping you from chasing your dreams, and how can you start shaking things up?

Action Steps:

1. **Dig Deep:** Grab a notebook or your phone and jot down the fears that are holding you back. Be real about what's keeping you stuck.

2. **Challenge Your Inner Critic:** Look at each fear you wrote down. Ask yourself, "Is this really true? What's the evidence for or against it?" Sometimes, just questioning those thoughts can make a world of difference.

3. **Take Tiny Steps:** Break your big dreams into bite-sized goals. Pick two small things you can do this week to move closer to what you want. It could be anything from updating your resume to having a chat with someone in your dream field.

4. **Reach Out:** Talk to friends, family, or anyone who gets you. Share what you're aiming for and ask for their support. You'd be surprised how many people want to cheer you on!

5. **Check Yourself:** At the end of the week, take a moment to reflect. What did you learn? What went well, and what needs tweaking? It's all about figuring out what works for you.

6. **Celebrate the Little Wins:** Don't wait for a huge breakthrough to celebrate. Every little step counts! Take a moment to acknowledge your progress and remind yourself that this journey is all about growth, not perfection.

s Aadi's journey comes to a close, you might be thinking that this is simply a fictional story, one crafted to inspire and provoke thought. But if we take a moment to look around us, not far, just in our everyday surroundings, we'll find countless stories like Aadi's. There are young, vulnerable individuals who face immense challenges, and yet, through perseverance, self-belief, and an unwavering spirit, they rise above their circumstances. They embrace their potential and, in their own way, defy gravity.

We looked around the city of Agra, where we live, and have been fortunate to witness many remarkable stories of resilience. However, today, we're excited to share just one of them, the inspiring journey of Priti. Having personally spoken to her for over two hours, we're indeed honored to share her story, a real-life example of resilience and determination. Priti, a talented young woman who, much like Aadi, faced rejections, judgments, and societal pressures, but never let them define her. She transformed her challenges into stepping stones toward success.

18

DANCING AGAINST THE ODDS

Priti's Gravity-Defying Story

Priti's Gravity-Defying Journey: A Story of Unyielding Passion and Perseverance

From the narrow, bustling streets of Agra, a city known for its grandeur in history, rose a girl named Priti, whose dreams were as vast as the open sky and as bright as the stars. She was born into a world where the odds were stacked against her, a world where poverty, hardship, and societal norms threatened to bury her dreams before they even took flight. Yet, like a seed pushing through the cracks in concrete, Priti defied gravity, rising above every challenge that life threw at her.

The Early Years: Seeds of Hope Amid Adversity

Priti's childhood was one of scarcity and struggle. With two younger siblings—one brother and one sister—she watched her father juggle odd jobs at retail stores, tea stalls, halwai shops, and even lottery counters. There were days when a simple meal felt like a luxury, and the constant fear of unpaid bills loomed large. Festivals, which should have been filled with joy and celebration, passed by in silence, marked only by the worry etched on her parents' faces.

Yet, amid these tough times, there was one gift her father gave that would change her life forever – an education in an English medium school. Though there were moments when they had to drop out due to a lack of funds, this exposure ignited a spark in Priti, one that would burn brighter with each passing day. While her peers were living carefree lives, Priti dreamed of transforming her family's situation, her love for her parents becoming the force that fueled her determination.

Inspired by dance performances on television, Priti found solace in movement. She would mimic the steps she saw on screen, and this blossomed into a passion that carried her through school dance competitions. By the time she reached grade seven, she had found her calling, she wanted to be a choreographer. But how could a young girl,

Priti's Parents

From the stage of dreams to the hearts of many—Priti, alongside her proud parents and talented troupe, shines bright as she shares her inspiring journey with the judges. A moment of triumph, love, and unbreakable spirit!

with no resources and no roadmap, pursue such a dream? The path was unclear, but the fire within her was unwavering.

The First Test: A Father's Accident and Priti's Resolve

Just when it seemed her dreams were taking shape, life threw its first real test her way. After completing her 10th grade, Priti's father was involved in a horrific accident, one so severe that it required extensive surgery and drained the family's already meager savings. The idea of continuing her education seemed impossible now, especially in a conservative household where girls were not encouraged to step outside and work. But Priti was not one to succumb to fate. She decided to take matters into her own hands.

With her brother working till late hours at a chemist's shop, earning just Rs. 2000 a month, Priti began offering tuition classes to small children in her neighborhood to fund her own education. Each day was a challenge, returning from school with no guarantee of food, rushing out to tutor kids, all the while managing her own studies. Yet, through the hardships, Priti discovered a deep truth: ***When you dream big and commit to your goals, the universe conspires to help you.***

The Dance Journey Begins: A Chance Encounter

One day, while giving tuition at a student's house, Priti stumbled upon a dance class, a chance encounter that would change her life. She yearned to join, but the fee—Rs. 500—was an insurmountable obstacle. So, she negotiated with the teacher, offering to bring friends along in exchange for a discounted rate. From here, her professional journey in Kathak began.

By the time she completed her 12th grade, Priti made a bold decision. She declined her acceptance at the prestigious Dayalbagh Educational Institute, choosing instead Agra College, where she would have more

Priti Singh
Dance Choreographer

time to pursue her dance passion. Her heart was set on her dream, and nothing—not even the lure of a prestigious college—could derail her.

The First Rejection: Dance Agra Dance

Priti's growing confidence led her to participate in the local competition, *Dance Agra Dance (DAD)*. She poured her heart and soul into her performance, only to be met with crushing rejection. 'We are NIL', she thought, as tears flowed uncontrollably. But true to her nature, Priti didn't give up. She learned the art of resilience, a lesson she would return to time and again throughout her journey.

Despite the setback, Priti forged ahead. Her confidence was bolstered by the unwavering support of her mother, her secret confidante. Together, they shielded her passion from her strict father, who would never have approved of a girl pursuing dance. But her resolve only strengthened. She knew she was on the right path, even if society was quick to judge.

Joining Akash Dance Academy: A New Chapter

The universe intervened once again when a friend introduced her to Akash Dance Academy in Sanjay Place, Agra, a place notorious for being unsafe for girls at the time. But Priti had no choice. She wanted to learn Hip-Hop, and Akash Sir, the academy's founder, saw potential in her. The fees, once again, were a barrier, but Priti's knack for negotiation shone through. She struck a deal, she would bring in more students in exchange for fee exemption. Thus began her training in Hip-Hop, and from there, she formed a troupe with Akash Sir, boys and girls, all united by their love for dance.

Priti and her troupe became a force to be reckoned with. They performed on local television and quickly gained a reputation in the city. Their performances were electric, and soon they were the team to

Kirron Kher

-Indian Actress, Television Personality, Entertainment Producer

Ye to mere golden buzzer wale ladke hai. Mujhe toh inka act hamesha accha lagta hai!

Crazy Hoppers from Agra you deserve to be the winners of IGT, I hope and pray! Aapane Jo Aaj Bharat ke sipahiyon ki shaan dikhai hai, ek army officer ki Beti Hun Main, itni proud hun, Meri rag rag mein is Desh ke liye Jo zinda-dili Jo ijjat, aur jo pyar daudta hai, Aaj Maine dekha! Salam hai aapko!

Inki Jo baitheen Hain chhoti Si choreographer, usko Salam zarur karna hai!

Bahut achcha kaam Kiya beta aapane. Bahut achcha, Very Well Done!

beat in every competition. But life, ever the tough taskmaster, wasn't done testing her yet.

The First IGT Journey: A Dream Delayed but Not Deterred

In 2014, Priti and her troupe auditioned for *India's Got Talent (IGT)*, the biggest platform for showcasing talent in India. A fully funded trip to Mumbai, stay in a luxurious hotel, and performing on a national stage felt like a dream come true. But fate played its cruel hand once more. They missed their train. Devastated, they rebooked and made it just in time for their performance. Their act was a success, earning them a cash prize of Rs. 11,000, and their photos flashed across media outlets. For the first time, her father saw her dance journey and felt immense pride.

But it wasn't all smooth sailing. They faced rejection in the judges' round of IGT. Though crushed, Priti refused to let it break her spirit. Her group fell apart, but she built it up again, piece by piece. Each rejection only fueled her desire to grow, to learn, to be better.

2016: The Golden Buzzer That Wasn't

In 2016, they auditioned again for IGT. This time, their performance received a standing ovation from the judges: Kirron Kher, Malaika Arora, and Karan Johar. Kirron Kher was moved to tears and fought for them to receive the golden buzzer. Getting the golden buzzer was a straight ticket to the semi-finals. All seemed to have gone right. Their happiness knew no bounds! But, unbelievably, once again, fate intervened, and even after days of endless wait, they didn't get the call to continue.

Priti cried for hours that day. The rejection was bitter, but she learned that every setback was a setup for a greater comeback. Once again, her team, demotivated and broken, dissolved. Half of the group members left, and the remaining needed her to lift them up. The fighter that she is, she rose to the challenge, rebuilding the team, yet again.

2018: The Aghori Act and the Golden Buzzer

By 2018, Priti had become a seasoned competitor. She returned to IGT with a stunning Aghori act that left the judges in awe. Kirron Kher screamed in delight, and this time, the golden buzzer was hers. She bypassed several rounds, soaring straight into the semi-finals, a remarkable achievement. Competing in IGT wasn't just about dance; it meant going head-to-head with magicians, stunt artists, musicians, and more. The stakes were high, but Priti's resolve was higher.

Though they didn't win, the experience taught her one invaluable lesson: *Always be ready for greatness, but never shy away from hard work.*

2021: Rising Again After COVID

And who said that success is linear? When the pandemic hit, everything came to a grinding halt. The troupe disbanded again. But like a hawk waiting for its prey, Priti stayed patient, and when the world reopened, they returned to IGT once more. In 2021, they received another golden buzzer, propelling them into the semi-finals. The competition was fiercer than ever, but Priti had mastered the art of perseverance. They didn't make it to the finals this time either.

As a reader you must be wondering that despite so many attempts at IGT, she didn't win the trophy! Then, what's the big deal about her journey?

Well, Priti's journey reveals a truth far more profound than victory: success is not confined to trophies or titles. Every attempt she made on that stage made her stronger in her resolve, refined her craft, and expanded her visibility. Though she did not win the coveted title, Priti's true victory lay in the impact she created beyond the competition.

Malaika Arora -Indian Actress and Dancer

You guys are beyond crazy. You all are unbelievable! If you guys win you will do IGT season 8 full justice! You guys deserve it!

She is a tiny little thing!

Vicky Kaushal -Indian Actor

Dharmendra

Manoj Muntashir

Badshah

Her craft and her determination caught the eye of renowned film directors and celebrity choreographers, who recognized not just her talent, but her spirit. Invitations began pouring in—from performing at international events to collaborating with celebrated artists. Priti's journey became a testament to the idea that sometimes the world's recognition matters more than a single competition's verdict.

She defied gravity by refusing to be defined by traditional success. She didn't give up. Instead, she kept moving, turning rejections into redirection. Today, her dance transcends borders, inspiring countless young dreamers to believe that success is not about winning a moment but about living your purpose, unapologetically and relentlessly.

In the end, Priti didn't need a trophy to prove her worth—her journey itself became her legacy. Through her art, she continues to inspire, reminding everyone that defying gravity isn't about reaching the top; it's about refusing to stay grounded when the world says you should.

You could follow her groups Priti Ke Parindey and Crazy Hoppers on:

Instagram @teampriti.official, YouTube @Pritikeparindey

Lessons for Life: Priti's Journey as a Beacon of Hope

After going through her life story, you'd agree that Priti's gravity-defying journey is far more than just a dance story. It's a profound lesson in life, one that teaches us about perseverance, passion, and the power of belief. Her story is a beacon of hope, lighting the way for dreamers everywhere. For parents, it's a lesson in nurturing aspirations, no matter how impossible they may seem. And for every young person, Priti's journey stands as proof that dreams can take flight even in the most unfavorable circumstances. Her reflections offer deep insights into what drives her and how her experiences have shaped the lessons she wishes to share with today's youth and parents alike. Here are some powerful life lessons we can draw from her experiences:

1. Resilience is the Wind Beneath the Wings

Just as a kite rises higher against the wind, Priti's journey shows us that adversity doesn't have to pull us down; instead, it can propel us forward. Her life was marked by countless rejections, from losing out in local competitions to facing setbacks at *India's Got Talent* (IGT). Yet, each of these failures became stepping stones on her path to success. Rather than being paralyzed by her disappointments, she embraced resilience, learning from each rejection and bouncing back stronger.

Like a river cutting through rock, not because of its power but because of its persistence, Priti's story reminds us that true strength lies not in avoiding difficulties but in navigating through them. For parents, it's a reminder to instill in their children the value of persistence, helping them understand that setbacks are temporary, and with patience and determination, anything is possible.

· LESSONS for LIFE ·
A Beacon of Hope

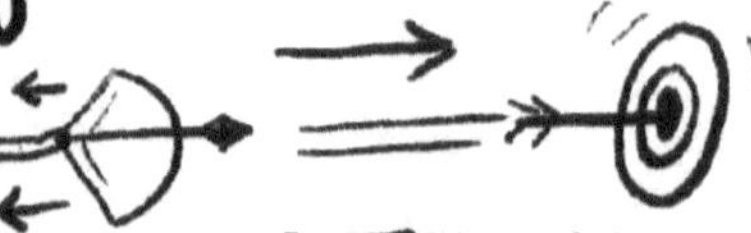

RESILIENCE
is the Wind beneath the Wings

Every SETBACK
is a Setup
for a Greater
COMEBACK

POWER
of SUPPORT
Families are silent Partners in Success

PASSION is the North Star that guide us through the darkest nig

DREAM BIG START SMALL KEEP GOING
SELF-BELIEF
The unshakable foundation of SUCCESS
Drawing ENERGY from CRITICISM
"logon ka kya hai, sab kuch bolenge"
Mujhe apne talent par poora VISHWAS! hain
KNOW your DRIVING FORCE
Talent ek cheez hain jo koi tumse nahin cheen sakta hain!
Parents: Support your children 200%
LIFE a DANCE of DREAMS

2. Every Setback is a Setup for a Greater Comeback

Priti's journey proves that setbacks are not the end. Rejection, criticism, and failure are all part of the path to greatness.

Throughout Priti's dance journey, she experienced numerous challenges, but she believed that every failure is a stepping stone to success. Every time her troupe fell apart, every time she was rejected on a national platform, she faced a crossroads. She could have chosen to quit, but she didn't. Instead, she chose to rebuild, rework, and refine her skills. This resilience became her superpower, demonstrating that setbacks are not dead ends but detours guiding us toward an even greater comeback.

Each rejection from IGT—whether it was missing her train in 2014, not getting the golden buzzer in 2016, or failing to advance in the finals in 2021—was painful. But Priti *learned to treat these moments as dress rehearsals for the grand stage.* She embraced failure not as a sign of weakness but as preparation for success, knowing perseverance will always pay off.

She believed, no matter how many times life knocks you down, it's how you get back up that defines your story. Priti's resolve to keep going despite countless rejections serves as a powerful example for anyone chasing a dream.

Parents can take away an essential message here: when your child fails or faces a setback, remind them that it's not the end of their journey. Instead, it's a lesson to be learned, a muscle to be strengthened. Failure is not something to be feared but something to be respected and used as a stepping stone toward success.

3. The Power of Support: Families are Silent Partners in Success

Priti's journey highlights the quiet, often unseen role that family support plays in the achievement of dreams. Her mother, a simple, uneducated woman, like a guardian angel, stood behind her with unwavering faith, even when societal norms and financial limitations threatened to extinguish Priti's aspirations. Though her father initially disapproved of her dancing, he later became her proudest supporter, demonstrating how transformative it can be for parents to believe in their children's potential.

Families act as the soil in which a child's dreams are planted. Like a sapling that needs water, sunlight, and care, dreams need the nourishment of encouragement, patience, and faith. The journey may be long, but with the backing of a supportive family, children can flourish even in the toughest environments. For parents, the lesson here is clear: stand by your children's dreams, even when they seem improbable. Your belief could be the fuel that keeps their dreams alive.

4. Passion is the North Star that Guides Us Through the Darkest Nights

Priti's decision to take up tuition work and her bold negotiation with the dance teacher show that when one door seems closed, you can always create your own window of opportunity.

Priti's love for dance was more than just a hobby, it was her lifeline. No matter how hard things got, her approach was always solution-oriented and not problem-oriented, and instinctively, she looked for solutions even when, apparently, there were none. No matter how many times her troupe fell apart or how many rejections she faced, her passion for dance never waned. This passion became her guiding light, helping her navigate through the toughest of times. It was her north star, the constant that kept her moving forward even when the road seemed impossible.

Her story underscores an important truth: when you have a passion that burns within you, it will carry you through the darkest nights. For young people, this is a reminder to hold on to what makes your heart beat faster. No matter how far-fetched or challenging your dreams may seem, passion will always show you the way. Parents, too, must recognize the importance of nurturing their children's passions, even if those passions don't align with traditional or 'safe' career paths.

5. Dream Big, Start Small, and Keep Going

No matter where you come from, it's your inner fire that will shape your future. Priti's passion for dance and desire to uplift her family was enough to spark her journey.

One of the greatest lessons from Priti's story is the importance of dreaming big despite circumstances, while taking small, deliberate steps forward. Her dream of becoming a choreographer was born in the small moments, mimicking TV dance steps, performing at school, offering tuition to fund her own education, and negotiating discounts for dance lessons. These were humble beginnings, but each small step brought her closer to her ultimate goal.

Dreams often seem unattainable from a distance, like distant mountains. But Priti's journey teaches us that when we break down our goals into smaller, manageable actions, we slowly but surely make progress. For parents, this is a reminder to encourage your children to take those small steps. Whether it's enrolling them in local classes, supporting them through competitions, or simply believing in their abilities, every small action counts toward a bigger vision.

6. Self-Belief: The Unshakable Foundation of Success

Amid all the rejections, tears, and setbacks, one thing remained constant in Priti's journey, her unshakable belief in herself. Even when others doubted her or when circumstances made it hard to keep going, she held on to the belief that she was destined for something greater. This self-belief became the foundation of her success.

Just as a tree stands tall because of its deep roots, Priti stood tall through adversity because her roots were grounded in self-confidence. For parents, the lesson here is to cultivate that self-belief in your children. Help them understand their worth, teach them to trust in their abilities, and remind them that they are capable of achieving greatness, no matter what obstacles lie in their path.

7. Drawing Energy from Criticism

In our conversation, Priti opened up about the strength she draws from the very people who have criticized her. '**Logon ka kya hai, sab kuch bolenge,**' Priti said, reflecting on how society judged her. Growing up, she was criticized for her short height, her appearance, and most notably, for joining boys in group dances, a big deal in her community. Many labeled her as *'characterless,'* assuming her decision to dance with boys was for fun, not understanding the passion and dedication she held for her craft.

But instead of letting this criticism crush her spirit, Priti used it as fuel to drive her ambitions. She developed an ironclad resolve to prove her detractors wrong. *'Mera bhi time aayega'*, she would tell herself, believing that her moment of success was just around the corner. Her journey wasn't just about dance, it became a mission to change perceptions, to defeat the narrow-minded views that had plagued her life.

Even today, people still judge Priti for her height and looks. Despite her success, some continue to take her lightly. But her focus never wavers. She has learned to tune out the negativity because her faith in her talent, skills, and passion remains unshakable. *"Mujhe apne talent par poora vishwaas hai,"* she declared with quiet confidence. She refuses to let others' judgments define her. Instead, she stays laser-focused on her goal, a lesson she wishes to pass on to others.

8. Know Your Driving Force

When asked what advice she would give to today's youth, Priti's message was simple but profound. *"Sabse pehle, apna driving force dhundho,"* she said. For her, it was the love for her parents and the desire to uplift her family's financial condition that gave her the energy to keep going, no matter the obstacles. Identifying this driving force is crucial, it gives meaning to your journey and keeps you grounded even during the toughest times.

"Goal clear hona chahiye," Priti emphasized. For her, having a clear goal was the key to navigating through the noise of life's distractions. Once your goal is clear, she says, everything else should revolve around

it. ***"Passion toh follow dil se hota hai,"*** she added, reminding us that true passion comes from the heart and cannot be faked. Her message is one of sincerity: be honest with yourself about what truly matters to you, and once you find that, pour your heart and soul into it.

With sharp focus, discipline, and unwavering determination, Priti believes that any hardship becomes easier to face. Even when people treat you poorly or life delivers rejections, those moments only serve to help you refine your strategy, plan your next move, and aim even higher. ***"Failure is unpredictable,"*** Priti said, acknowledging that setbacks are inevitable. But instead of fearing failure, she encourages young people to remain prepared for it at all times.

"Talent ek cheez hai jo koi tumse nahi cheen sakta," Priti firmly believes. No matter what happens, no one can take away the skills and abilities you've worked hard to develop. While others may withdraw their support, remember her mantra: ***"Mehnat toh mujhe hi karni hai."*** You must always be self-dependent. No one will walk your path for you, so develop the strength to push forward on your own.

"Bachchon ki tarah, hamesha masoom aur hopeful raho," she advised, comparing the spirit of a dreamer to the innocence of a child. Like a child who remains endlessly hopeful and curious, Priti believes that maintaining this sense of wonder and optimism is key to overcoming the challenges life throws at you.

9. Parents: Support Your Children 200%

Priti's advice to parents is clear: let your children follow their passions. ***"Unn ko jo karna hai, karne do"*** she urged. "It's important," she says, "for parents to support their children with everything they have,— ***Supporting them 200%***"—and to not impose their own desires or expectations on their kids." Priti believes that while parents should offer guidance and suggestions, they should never become overbearing or controlling. ***"Guide karo, suggest karo, par haawi mat hona,"*** she said, emphasizing that parents must allow their children the freedom to chart their paths while offering the necessary support from the sidelines.

10. Life: A Dance of Dreams

Priti's journey is more than just a dance story; it's a testament to the human spirit's ability to rise above, to defy gravity even when the world tells you to stay grounded. Her life is a dance of dreams, where every step, leap, and fall is part of a larger performance. For parents and children alike, Priti's story is a call to action: ***Dream big, believe in yourself, and never stop moving forward.***

Like a dancer who finds grace even in the stumble, Priti's life teaches us to embrace the challenges, to keep pushing forward, and to remember that no matter how many times we fall, we are always one step closer to soaring.

Her firm belief: The journey is never over

Even when you reach new heights, life will keep testing you. It's your resilience and unwavering belief in your dreams that will push you to new levels of success.

Parallels of Perseverance: Aadi and Priti's Gravity-Defying Journeys

In life, we often come across stories of resilience, where the heroes rise above their circumstances to carve their own paths. You've now read two such stories: Aadi's fictional journey and the real-life story of Priti, a choreographer who defied gravity to emerge as a beacon of hope. Though their worlds may seem different, Aadi navigating the emotional landscape of personal growth, and Priti battling societal judgments to achieve her dreams, their journeys are marked by common threads of perseverance, determination, and the relentless pursuit of a dream.

Starting with a Struggle: The Early Years

Both Aadi and Priti began their journeys in challenging circumstances. Aadi, grappling with internal conflicts, struggled to find self-acceptance. Priti, on the other hand, faced the harsh realities of financial instability and societal constraints.

Priti grew up in a home where the weight of poverty was felt daily. Her father, unable to maintain a stable job, took up various odd jobs just to make ends meet. Her childhood was punctuated with the struggle for basic necessities, unpaid electricity bills, no festival celebrations, and the absence of regular meals. But despite this, she held on to her one treasure: the love for her family and her burning desire to change her family's circumstances. She, like Aadi, held a vision that life could be different.

Lesson for Us: No matter how grim the start, it's our internal drive, that 'hunger' for a better life, which propels us to dream. Just as Aadi was nudged toward self-discovery, Priti's hardships ignited her passion to not just survive but transform her world.

The Moment of Realization

For both Aadi and Priti, there came a moment of realization, a turning point when they knew their path would be different.

For Aadi, this moment came when he recognized the impact of negative internal dialogues on his well-being. It was a shift from victimhood to taking control of his own narrative, choosing happiness and growth over self-doubt.

For Priti, the realization came when she saw dancers on TV and began mimicking them. Dancing was her joy, her escape, and ultimately, her dream. Despite not knowing how, she started dreaming of becoming a choreographer. But life wasn't easy for her. After her 10th grade, her father's accident drained the family's finances. With no money for her education, the dream seemed distant. Yet, like Aadi, Priti took matters into her own hands.

She began giving tuition classes to fund her 11th and 12th grades, squeezing out time to follow her passion. In a student's house, she discovered a local dance class that would change her life forever. Despite financial struggles, she managed to negotiate her way into the class, marking the beginning of her professional Kathak journey.

Lesson for Us: The first step in defying gravity is recognizing what holds us down and deciding, against all odds, to rise above it. For Aadi, it was his own self-doubt; for Priti, it was financial and societal limitations.

Facing Rejections and Rising Stronger

Rejection is often seen as a roadblock, but for both Aadi and Priti, it was a stepping stone to resilience.

Aadi's journey was fraught with setbacks, but each time, he learned to view them as opportunities for growth. He realized that his internal battles and rejections were merely challenges to be overcome. He reframed his internal dialogues and moved forward with more determination each time.

Priti faced similar challenges. After excelling at local dance competitions, she set her sights on the national stage. Her participation in the *Dance Agra Dance* competition was a stepping stone toward *India's Got Talent* (IGT), her ultimate dream. But her first big test ended in rejection. After hours of practice, when the results were announced, it wasn't her name called. She locked herself in a room, crying her heart out, feeling the weight of disappointment.

But Priti, like Aadi, chose not to give up. She viewed the rejection as a lesson, realizing that she needed to sharpen her skills. She sought out a new teacher, joined a challenging dance academy where boys dominated, and slowly built a new team. Her resolve hardened with each setback. Her group faced multiple rejections in *India's Got Talent*, even making it to the semi-finals but losing in the final stages multiple times. Yet, each loss only fueled her fire to improve and aim higher.

Lesson for Us: Rejection is not the end; it's a moment of learning. For both Aadi and Priti, each 'no' became a reason to work harder, improve, and keep moving forward. When we embrace setbacks, they become lessons, not barriers.

Support Systems and Self-Reliance

Neither Aadi nor Priti could have survived their journeys without the support of loved ones. But equally important was their self-reliance.

For Aadi, the guidance of his mother became a light in the dark. Her love and support gave him the confidence to face his struggles. Yet, he knew that the real work had to be done by him. He had to own his path, accept responsibility for his growth, and take charge of his happiness.

Priti, too, had the unwavering support of her mother, who silently encouraged her to pursue her passion. Her mother was her confidante, keeping her dance dreams a secret from her father, who would have disapproved. However, like Aadi, Priti knew that her journey was her own. She had to fund her education, manage the hardships at home, and fight societal judgments, all while holding onto her dream.

Lesson for Us: Support systems—be it family, friends, or mentors—are vital. But ultimately, success is a result of self-reliance. As Priti says, *"Mehnat toh mujhe hi karni hai"* the hard work has to be done by us.

Clarity of Vision and the Power of Focus

One of the strongest parallels between Aadi and Priti is their unwavering focus on their goals.

Aadi's journey was about gaining clarity, learning to focus on what truly mattered to him, whether it was self-acceptance or reframing his mindset to live a happier, more fulfilled life.

Priti's journey was similar in its singularity of vision. Despite societal judgments, rejections, and even the physical challenge of her short height, she remained focused on one thing, becoming a successful dancer and choreographer. Her mantra, ***"Goal clear hona chahiye,"*** is a powerful message for anyone aiming to defy gravity. She built her life around that goal, ensuring that every step she took brought her closer to her dream.

Lesson for Us: When you have a clear goal and focus your energy on it, distractions fall away. Both Aadi and Priti remind us that clarity of purpose is the foundation of success.

Lessons for Parents

Priti's advice to parents is a reflection of her own journey: ***"Support your kids 200%."*** In her words, parents should guide their children but not overshadow them with control.

Aadi's journey, too, highlights the importance of a nurturing environment. His mother's unconditional support allowed him to explore, fall, and rise again.

Lesson for Parents: Encourage your children to pursue their passions, provide them with the emotional and practical support they need, and, most importantly, trust them to navigate their own paths.

Conclusion: Defying Gravity, Together

The journeys of Aadi and Priti show us that defying gravity isn't about one giant leap, it's about the small, consistent steps taken despite adversity. Whether it's reframing negative thoughts, like Aadi, or using criticism as fuel for success, like Priti, the lesson is the same: you have the power to rise above your circumstances, no matter how daunting they may seem.

Priti's story of rejection and success, paired with Aadi's journey of self-discovery, reminds us that the road to greatness is never easy, but it's always worth it. In both their lives, we find examples of how determination, self-reliance, and unwavering focus can transform even the hardest obstacles into stepping stones for success.

So, whether you're a parent nurturing your child's dreams or a young adult like Aadi or Priti, take heart. Your gravity-defying journey is just beginning. Keep your goal clear, work hard, and remember, success is not about avoiding failure, but about refusing to let it define you.

FINAL REFLECTION

A Personal Note of Empowerment

As we come to the end of this journey together, both of us (Drishti & Neha) want to take a moment to express our deepest gratitude for allowing us to share this space with you. This book isn't just a collection of strategies or theories, it is a reflection of our experiences, lessons, and truths. We have walked beside you, hoping to empower you to embrace your own unique journey.

For parents and youth alike, it's important to remember: *the power to change your life lies within you.* Whether you are a parent learning to communicate better with your child or a young person navigating the complexities of life, growth begins when you make the decision to take ownership of your story.

A Call to Action

We believe that knowledge without action doesn't bring about transformation. So, here's our challenge to you: don't let this book end when you close it. Instead, let it mark the beginning of a new chapter in your life.

For Parents: Start those difficult conversations with your children. Listen without judgment. Be the guiding light that helps them rise above challenges rather than someone who adds to the weight they carry.

For Youth: Understand that your path may not always be clear, and that's okay. What's important is that you take the first step, however small, and trust yourself to navigate the rest. And remember, consistency is the key!

Both of you—parents and children—have the potential to create relationships built on mutual respect, love, and empowerment. So, we urge you to act now. Use the tools we've shared, start your 30-Day Challenge, and reflect on your inner strengths.

A Vision for the Future

Imagine a future where you and your loved ones communicate freely, where guilt, fear, and judgment no longer hold power over your relationships. Imagine a world where each family fosters growth, resilience, and emotional intelligence.

This future isn't a distant dream; it is within reach. It begins with small, consistent actions. It starts with you, right now. The shifts you make today will shape the world for generations to come. It will ripple through your family, your community, and beyond. You have the power to inspire this change.

Acknowledgment of the Journey

Growth is rarely easy. There will be moments when it feels like two steps forward and one step back. This is a part of the process. In those moments, remind yourself: setbacks are not failures. They are opportunities to reflect, learn, and course-correct.

You are stronger than you think, and your potential is limitless. Whether you're a parent trying to break free from old habits or a young person feeling uncertain about the future, remember, it's okay to stumble, as long as you keep moving forward.

Patience, Persistence, and Self-Compassion are your allies. Lean on them. Know that every effort you make is a step toward becoming the best version of yourself.

An Invitation for Reflection

As we part ways, we invite you to take a few moments to reflect on your journey so far:

1. What have you learned about yourself through this book?

2. What are the key insights you will implement immediately?

3. What is one thing you will do differently today that could create a ripple effect in your life?

4. Write these thoughts down. Allow yourself the time to process, to commit, and to celebrate your growth. Your life is your story, and every new choice you make is a line in your personal narrative. You hold the pen. You write the next chapter.

THE JOURNEY CONTINUES

Stay Connected

Dear reader, this is not an ending, but a new beginning – a fresh start full of possibilities. Both of us are rooting for you, just as we have been throughout these pages. We believe in you, and we hope that after reading this book, you believe in yourself just as much.

Let this book be a guide, a companion, and a reminder that *you can defy your gravity.*

And since a book is not an ending, we would love to stay connected with each of you. So, please feel free to interact with us on our website:

1. **Your Story Matters: Inspire and Empower**

   We invite you all to share your own stories, thoughts, or takeaways from the book with us on <u>brandingyourgrowth.com</u>, and let's inspire others together!

Example:

Share with us the story of how you've overcome challenges, reframed failure, or found resilience in tough times?

2. **Your Voice, Your Choice: Stories That Inspire**

   In this segment, feel free to share with us real-life stories that you find could inspire many others. We will select the best ones, and they'll find a proud space on our website and on our social media handles for the benefit of many others.

Example: Visit our website, click on the link <u>brandingyourgrowth.com</u>, share and help us bring more inspiring stories to light.

With love and encouragement,

Neha & Drishti

ANNEXURES

Annexure A: A Heart-to-Heart

Your Questions, Our Answers

Welcome to our comprehensive Chit Chat in this Q&A section! After personal conversations with some parents and some young boys & girls, we've gathered 30 most pressing questions, spanning a wide range of topics from communication, education, to relationships, and beyond. Together, we'll explore these concerns and offer insights from our perspectives, to help both parents and youth navigate their unique journeys.

<u>Communication</u>

Question 1:

Parent: "How can I improve communication with my teenager who refuses to open up? I feel like I'm always walking on eggshells around them."

Neha:

Improving communication starts with creating a safe, non-judgmental environment. Show genuine interest in their interests, listen actively without interrupting, and avoid giving unsolicited advice initially. Sometimes, simply being present and patient can make a significant difference.

Drishti:

Thinking from my perspective when I was in my teens, feeling heard without judgment is crucial. Sometimes, I didn't want any advice or a list of action points… just someone I could talk to freely. I guess parents could start by engaging in activities together regularly that don't feel like formal conversations, like cooking or playing board games, or just about anything else that you could bond over. For me, such relaxed settings have always made it easier for me to open up naturally.

Question 2:

Youth: "I find it hard to talk to my parents about my problems. They never seem to understand."

Drishti:

It can be tough when it feels like your parents aren't on the same page, especially when you need them the most. Try to find a calm time to express how you feel. Remember, no one can love us more or think for us more than our parents. That being a fact, trust in their love. If they don't seem to understand you, it's certainly not intentional. They may not realize that they are doing anything wrong.

So, you go and take the initiative to express your feelings. Don't accuse them. Use "I" statements, like "I feel overwhelmed when…" to communicate your feelings without sounding accusatory. In my opinion, this should be the case for deep conversations you have with anyone, including your parents.

Neha:

That's an amazing thought, Drishti! In reciprocation, as parents, we must encourage open dialogue by validating our child's feelings. We must let them know it's okay to feel the way they do and that we're there to support them.

Question 3:

Parent: "My child spends too much time on their phone. How can I address this without causing conflict?"

Neha:

What's most important here is modeling the right behavior. As a family, parents included, we must set clear and reasonable boundaries around phone usage. And while doing so, it's best to involve your child in creating these rules to ensure they feel respected and heard. Encourage alternative activities that interest them, such as sports or hobbies and whenever time permits, do these together. I remember, as a kid, Drishti joined a fun Bollywood dance class. Some of the mothers, me included, joined the same batch. We used to stand right behind in the last row, bonding with our kids, and subtly supporting them while they learned something new. It also indirectly assured them of our presence in their lives.

Drishti:

Oh, I remember that. That was adorable. We used to have fun practicing those songs at home too. Coming to the point, it helps when parents understand that smartphones are integral to our social lives and learning. Instead of outright bans and strict rules that could maybe draw us away from them, I think negotiating specific times for phone use can be more effective. Also, showing interest in what they're doing online can build trust while respecting their privacy.

Question 4:

Youth: "I feel like my parents don't respect my opinions. What can I do?"

Drishti:

Start by expressing your feelings calmly and respectfully. Let them know you value their perspective but also want your opinions to be heard. Sometimes, demonstrating responsibility can earn you more respect over time.

Neha:

According to me, respect is a two-way street. Parents definitely need to show their children that they respect their children's opinions. If you feel that they don't respect your opinion, firstly talk to them, as Drishti said, but then, also take a minute to introspect and see what could be the reason behind that, maybe discuss this openly with them. You'll be surprised how a simple conversation like this could foster mutual respect.

Education and Career

Question 5:

Parent: "How can I support my child in choosing the right career path without imposing my own expectations?"

Neha:

"Encourage your child to explore their interests and strengths from an early age. Provide resources and opportunities for them to gain experience in various fields. Maintain open conversations about their aspirations and support their decisions, even if they differ from your expectations and society's norms. As a parent, the most supportive thing you could do is to believe in them. Trust me, children are capable of performing miracles on their own if they know that you believe in them."

Drishti:

"It's empowering to have parents who support your interests. Children must share their passions and concerns openly and seek their parents' advice when needed. Remember, it's your journey, and it's okay to take time to find what truly excites you. In my case, I definitely discussed my choices with my parents and my teachers too. However, they encouraged me to pick what I was truly interested in. For me, when things were difficult and I was under pressure, be it at school or otherwise, the one thing that mom used to say, and it just lightened my heart was, 'Just leave it, Drishti. Your life is a dynamic stream of exploring your true passion.' This just propelled me to conquer whatever challenge was bothering me."

Question 6:

Youth: "I'm unsure about what I want to study in college. How can I make this decision?"

Drishti:

"Take the time to explore different subjects through online courses, internships, projects, or part-time jobs. Reflect on what activities make you feel engaged and fulfilled. Talk to people who have been where you are now. Also, there is no 'perfect' choice when it comes to choosing your college major. You can always shift if what you opt for isn't your calling."

Neha:

"Encourage your child to explore various options and provide guidance without pressure. Consider career counseling services that can help identify strengths and interests to inform their decision."

Question 7:

Parent: "My child is struggling academically despite their efforts. How can I help them succeed?"

Neha:

"Identify the root cause of their struggles, whether it's learning difficulties, lack of interest, or external factors. Collaborate with teachers to create a support plan and consider tutoring or additional resources to help them improve. Sometimes, they might be struggling because they are studying the wrong stream, so it's always a good option to evaluate their talents and then help them academically. Every child is different and precious because of that."

Drishti:

"It's important to stay positive and focus on your strengths. Seek help when needed and don't be afraid to ask questions or request extra support from teachers. Don't get disheartened if a teacher refuses to help despite your request. Find someone else and, most importantly, talk to your parents; they'll help find a way. But remember, everyone learns differently. So, it's okay if there are struggles. Focus on finding the way out; you are your best shot at learning. Also, creating a timetable and enjoying the process helps learning better."

<u>Parenting Challenges</u>

Question 8:

Parent: "How can I balance being a supportive parent while also setting firm boundaries?"

Neha:

"Like I said earlier, open communication with your children should be introduced very early in life. Kids are very open to logic and understanding. Clearly communicate your expectations and the reasons behind them. Show empathy and understanding, but also enforce the boundaries respectfully. It's a balance of being both nurturing and authoritative. And remember, consistency is key."

Drishti:

"Understanding that boundaries are a form of care can help. When the parents explain the "why" behind rules, boundaries feel more reasonable and easier to accept."

Question 9:

Youth: "I disagree with my parents' decisions for my future. How can I express my views without causing arguments?"

Drishti:

"When you're having tough conversations, the best approach is to stay calm and respectful. Take the time to clearly explain what you're thinking and why you might disagree, but try to avoid turning it into a confrontation. Instead, focus on having a constructive dialogue where both sides can be heard.

"It's just as important to listen as it is to speak. Hear their perspective, even if you don't agree, and try to understand where they're coming from. When both sides are open and willing to talk things through, it makes it a lot easier to find some common ground and move forward without unnecessary conflict."

Neha:

"Try to keep conversations respectful so everyone can share their thoughts openly. Let your child express their feelings, and make sure to validate what they're saying, it helps them feel heard. At the same time, you can calmly explain your own concerns and where you're coming from. That way, it's more of a balanced conversation where both sides understand each other."

Question 10:

Parent: "How can I help my child develop good study habits without being overbearing?"

Neha:

"Set up a structured environment with a specific spot for studying and try to stick to consistent routines. It's also important to encourage breaks and maintain a good balance between work and free time. Be there to support them and provide any resources they need, but avoid hovering or micromanaging their study time, it helps them take ownership of their work."

Drishti:

"Having a quiet, organized space really makes a difference. Plus, when you know your parents trust you to manage your own time, it can be super motivating. It's also key to have a routine that includes time to unwind and enjoy your hobbies, balance is everything!"

Question 11:

Youth: "I feel pressured by my parents to achieve high grades. How can I cope with this stress?"

Drishti:

"View the situation objectively and be open to understanding your parents' perspective too before you talk to your parents about how you're feeling and let them know if you're feeling pressured. It's important they understand what you're going through. Don't hesitate to lean on friends, counselors, or mentors for support when it comes to managing stress. Focus on your own journey, setting goals that are realistic for *you*, not based on anyone else's expectations. Taking things step-by-step can make it all feel more manageable."

Neha:

"Acknowledge your child's efforts and emphasize that their well-being is more important than grades. It's important for them to focus more on learning, exploring more options so that they can figure out exactly what they would like to pursue in the long-term. This way, they'll be intrinsically motivated and you'll see them happy and achieving too. Therefore, it's important to encourage a healthy perspective on success and failure and provide reassurance that you support them regardless of academic outcomes."

<u>Youth Self-Development</u>

Question 12:

Parent: "How can I encourage my child to build self-confidence?"

Neha:

"Give your child plenty of opportunities to try different activities and find things they're good at, it could be sports, art, music, or even something completely unexpected. When you praise them, focus on the effort they're putting in, not just on the final outcome; they learn that hard work and persistence matter just as much as success.

"Encourage them to step outside their comfort zone and take on new challenges, even if they're a bit nervous. It's important to let them make their own decisions and figure things out for themselves. Sure, they might stumble along the way, but those experiences help them learn and grow. Letting them make mistakes can be a valuable lesson in itself!"

Drishti:

"I remember when I was younger, my parents let me try all sorts of activities, whether it was dance, art, or even sports. They gave me the freedom to explore, and it really helped me figure out what I enjoyed and where my strengths were. But what really made a difference was that they didn't just praise me for winning or being the best at something. They always focused on how much effort I was putting in, even if the outcome wasn't perfect.

"And yeah, sometimes I'd mess up, but those moments taught me a lot. One thing that helped me grow was being able to make decisions for myself. My parents let me learn from my mistakes, and even though it wasn't always easy, those experiences made me more confident in the long run."

Question 13:

Youth: "I struggle with self-esteem issues. What steps can I take to improve my self-worth?"

Drishti:

"One thing that really helped me was learning to focus on my strengths and accomplishments, even the small ones. It's easy to get caught up in what's going wrong, but taking time to recognize what you're doing right can change your whole mindset. I also made sure to surround myself with supportive people, friends and family who lift me up and make me feel good about myself. Especially when you are doing well and are happy, there could be a few bullies in school or at professional setups who will always try to discourage you by creating self-doubt. Be mindful of such people around you. Trust yourself and your loved ones, especially your parents.

"Another big thing for me was practicing self-compassion. I had to remind myself that it's okay to make mistakes and that I don't need to be perfect. Challenging negative self-talk was huge, too. Whenever I caught myself thinking things like, 'I'm not good enough' or 'I can't do this,' I'd try to flip it and remind myself of all the things I *can* do. It takes practice, but over time, it really makes a difference."

Neha:

"Like I always say, one of the best things you can do for your child is to encourage activities that really showcase their strengths and interests. It's all about finding what they love and helping them explore it! Whether it's sports, art, music, or even something like reading or writing, when kids engage in activities that excite them, it can really boost their confidence.

"And let's talk about praise, make it genuine and specific! Instead of just saying, 'Good job,' try to highlight exactly what they did well. For instance, if they painted a beautiful picture, you might say, 'I love how you used those colors! You really have an eye for detail.' This kind of praise goes a long way. It helps them understand what they're doing right and encourages them to keep going.

"One thing to keep in mind is to avoid comparing them to others. Every child is unique and has their own journey. Instead of saying, 'Why can't you be more like your friend who plays the piano?' focus on their personal progress. Celebrate their achievements, no matter how small they seem.

"Another effective way to boost their self-esteem is by helping them set and achieve personal goals. Start with small, achievable goals, maybe it's finishing a book, learning a new skill, or even just improving in a subject they find challenging. When they accomplish these goals, it reinforces the idea that they can succeed and gives them a sense of pride. It's about nurturing their growth and making sure they feel supported every step of the way."

Question 14:

Parent: "How can I help my child develop good decision-making skills?"

Neha:

"Again, my first word would be the same. Please encourage your kids to get involved in activities that they want to do and are also good at. For instance, Drishti has always loved music. From the day she was born, she would instantly sleep listening to the song "Dur". Then again, at a young age, we noticed how happy she was while practicing her songs, piano, tabla, sitar, or performing in front of a crowd. So, we made sure to support her passion by enrolling her in music classes and giving her plenty of opportunities to showcase her talent, whether it was in school performances or a variety of stage show events.

"Next, praise them. But the caution here is not to praise them for the sake of it; make it genuine and specific! They'd love to hear feedback that's very genuine and personal. Instead of just saying, 'Good job,' I'd point out exactly what she did well. After one of her performances, I told her, 'I loved how you sang those high notes effortlessly! You really captured the audience's attention with your energy!' This, kind of targeted praise, helped her believe in her decision-making skills and motivated her to keep pushing herself.

"Having made your own decision doesn't mean each time it's going to work. So, we urged her to cheer for others and realize that everyone likes to win at some point. And so, sometimes, one should be happy to celebrate others' happiness. So, while she learned to make her own choices and focus on her personal progress, we celebrated her achievements, no matter how small they might have seemed."

Drishti:

"Making decisions, even mistakes, is part of growing up. It helps you understand what works and what doesn't. Seek advice when needed, but trust your instincts and learn from each experience."

Question 15:

Youth: "I want to set personal goals but don't know where to start. How can I effectively set and achieve them?"

Drishti:

"Start by identifying what matters most to you. Break down your goals into smaller, manageable steps and set deadlines for each. Track your progress and adjust your plans as needed. Celebrate your achievements along the way."

Neha:

"Encourage your child to set SMART goals: Specific, Measurable, Achievable, Relevant, and Time-bound. Provide tools like planners or apps to help them stay organized and motivated."

Question 16:

Parent: "How can I teach my child resilience in the face of setbacks?"

Neha:

"Model resilience by handling your own setbacks gracefully. Encourage your child to view challenges as opportunities to grow. Teach problem-solving skills and provide support without taking over, allowing them to navigate difficulties independently."

Drishti:

"Resilience is built through overcoming challenges. When you face setbacks, try to find the lesson or the silver lining. It's important to stay positive and persistent, even when things get tough."

Question 17:

Youth: "I have trouble staying motivated. What strategies can help me stay on track with my goals?"

Drishti:

"Identify what truly inspires you and keep that vision in mind. Break your goals into smaller tasks and reward yourself for completing them. Surround yourself with supportive people and stay flexible, adjust your plans if needed to stay motivated."

Neha:

"Finding your 'why' behind each goal can boost motivation. Encourage your child to visualize their success and remind them of their progress regularly. Supportive environments and positive reinforcement can also keep motivation high."

Technology and Social Media

Question 18:

Parent: "How can I ensure my child uses technology and social media responsibly?"

Neha:

"Set clear guidelines and discuss the potential risks and benefits of technology use. Encourage balanced usage by promoting offline activities and setting limits on screen time. Monitor their online activities while respecting their privacy."

Drishti:

"Understanding the importance of digital well-being is key. Use social media mindfully, limit screen time, and engage in real-life interactions. It's also important to be critical of the content you consume and share online."

Question 19:

Youth: "I feel overwhelmed by social media and its impact on my self-image. How can I manage this?"

Drishti:

"Take regular breaks from social media to focus on real-life connections and activities. Curate your feed to include positive and inspiring content. Remember that social media often portrays an idealized version of life, which isn't always reality. Focus more on getting feedback about yourself from a selected group of people who care for you."

Neha:

"Encourage open discussions about the pressures of social media. Help your child understand the difference between online personas and real life, and promote activities that build self-esteem outside of digital platforms."

Question 20:

Parent: "My child is addicted to their smartphone. What can I do to help them reduce their screen time?"

Neha:

"Implement screen-free zones or times, such as during meals or before bedtime. Encourage alternative activities that interest them, like sports, reading, or creative hobbies. Lead by example by managing your own screen time effectively."

Drishti:

"Find a balance by setting specific times for phone use and sticking to them. Engage in activities that don't involve screens and communicate with friends in person to reduce dependency on digital interactions."

Question 21:

Youth: "I want to use social media for my passion projects. How can I do this effectively without it taking over my life?"

Drishti:

"Set specific goals for your social media use and allocate dedicated time for managing your projects. Use tools to schedule posts and track engagement efficiently. Maintain a healthy balance by prioritizing offline activities and self-care."

Neha:

"Support your child's creative endeavors on social media while ensuring they maintain a balanced lifestyle. Encourage them to set boundaries and monitor their online presence to prevent it from becoming overwhelming."

<u>Relationships</u>

Question 22:

Youth: "I'm having trouble making friends. What can I do to build meaningful relationships?"

Drishti:

"Engage in activities and communities that align with your interests. Be open and approachable, and show genuine interest in others. Building friendships takes time, so be patient and persistent in your efforts. And at the end of the day, you need to be your own best friend, so don't be afraid of being with yourself."

Neha:

"Encourage your child to join clubs, sports, or groups that interest them. Social skills can be developed through practice, so they can be supported in stepping out of their comfort zone gradually. Model more social behavior at home, which will make it easier for the child to transfer the same skills while making friends."

Question 23:

Youth: "I'm experiencing peer pressure to engage in activities I'm uncomfortable with. How can I handle this?"

Drishti:

"Assert your boundaries firmly and confidently. Surround yourself with friends who respect your choices and support your values. It's okay to say no and remove yourself from situations that make you uncomfortable."

Neha:

"Teach your child strategies to resist peer pressure, such as having prepared responses and choosing friends who respect their decisions. Encourage them to prioritize their well-being over fitting in."

Motivation and Goal-Setting

Question 24:

Youth: "I have big dreams but feel like they're unattainable. How can I stay motivated to achieve them?"

Drishti:

"Break down your big dreams into smaller, actionable goals. Create a timeline and track your progress. Surround yourself with supportive people and remind yourself why these dreams matter to you."

Neha:

"Encourage your child to visualize their goals and maintain a positive outlook. Provide resources and support to help them navigate obstacles and stay committed to their aspirations. The biggest change in their mindset comes from the faith you show in them, so make sure you help them follow through with a disciplined routine with confidence."

Question 25:

Youth: "I often procrastinate and struggle to stay focused. What strategies can help me overcome this?"

Drishti:

"Try setting up a schedule that breaks your day into specific times for work and breaks. Something like the Pomodoro Technique works really well. Focus for 25 minutes, then take a short break. It helps you stay on track without burning out. And honestly, cutting out distractions is a game-changer. Set up a space where you can really focus, and set small, achievable goals for each session. It makes everything feel more manageable!"

Neha:

"Helping your child develop good time management skills and get into a routine can make a huge difference. It's all about finding what works for them. Maybe start by helping them figure out what distractions they need to cut back on, whether it's their phone, TV, or something else. You can also give them tools to stay organized, like a planner or an app. Something that helps them keep track of everything in one place can really boost their focus and productivity."

Question 26:

Parent: "My child sets high goals but gets discouraged easily. How can I support their perseverance?"

Neha:

"Teach them to view setbacks as learning opportunities. Encourage resilience by celebrating their efforts and progress, not just the end results. Provide a supportive environment where they feel safe to take risks and make mistakes."

Drishti:

"When things don't go the way you hoped, it's super important to keep a positive attitude. I know it's easier said than done, but surrounding yourself with people who lift you up really makes a difference. And don't forget to remind yourself of all the things you've already achieved, those little wins can keep you motivated when things get tough."

Question 27:

Youth: "I'm struggling to find my passion. How can I discover what I truly love?"

Drishti:

"Honestly, don't be afraid to try out a bunch of different things, whether it's hobbies, subjects, or activities. You won't know what clicks until you give it a shot! Pay attention to what makes you feel excited, like you actually look forward to doing it. That's usually a good sign you're onto something. And seriously, it's totally okay if it takes time to find your passion. I've gone through phases where I've tried different things, and it's all part of figuring out what really feels right for you. In fact, currently, I'm also going through that phase."

Neha:

"As a parent myself, I would say one of the best things you can do is encourage your child to try all sorts of experiences. Let them explore and see what really brings them joy. It could be anything—sports, art, music, coding—whatever makes them excited. By giving them the chance to dive into different interests, you're helping them figure out what they're truly passionate about. And the best part? They'll start to discover what makes them happy and fulfilled on their terms."

Question 28:

Parent: "How can I help my child maintain a healthy work-life balance?"

Neha:

"Drishti & I have always been talking about time management and setting priorities. It's something we all struggle with, right? I encourage her to figure out what really needs to get done first and not to overwhelm herself by trying to do everything at once. But I also remind her how important it is to take breaks and do things that she enjoys. Whether it's a hobby, spending time with friends, or just relaxing, those moments are just as important as work or study.

"And honestly, I try to model this myself. I know if Drishti sees me constantly stressed and overworked, it's not sending the best message. So I make sure to take time for myself, too, whether it's reading, going for a walk, trekking, holidaying with friends, or just having a quiet cup of tea. When our kids see us balancing things, it sets a good example for them to follow."

Drishti:

"Yes, balancing work and personal life is super important for your well-being. I've had to learn that it's okay to set boundaries around when I'm working or studying. Once that time is up, I make sure to give myself space to relax or do something fun. Whether it's hanging out with friends, watching a show, or just chilling, taking time for yourself is just as important as getting stuff done. It's all about making sure you don't burn out while still staying on top of your goals."

Question 29:

Youth: "I feel overwhelmed by my long-term goals. How can I stay motivated for the future?"

Drishti:

"Focus on what's right in front of you by setting short-term goals that help you get closer to your bigger vision. Break it down into steps that feel doable right now. And seriously, celebrate those small wins along the way – they keep you motivated! Also, whenever things get tough or you feel stuck, remind yourself of why your goals matter to you. Keeping that *'why'* in mind really helps keep the excitement alive."

Neha:

"As a mom, I always encourage breaking big goals down into smaller, more manageable chunks. It's less overwhelming that way, and it helps you focus on what needs to be done right now. I do this with Drishti all the time, whether it's her projects or something she's working on personally.

"We regularly check in to see how things are going and adjust the plan if needed. Life happens, right? It's okay to make changes along the way. One thing I've learned is that keeping a positive outlook is so important. It helps you stay motivated, especially when things get tough. I also remind Drishti—and myself, really—of why we're doing what we're doing. Staying connected to that 'why' keeps us going in the long run."

Question 30:

Parent: "With so many distractions today, from social media to intense academics, how can parents ensure they remain connected with their children?"

Neha:

"To stay connected despite social media and academic pressures, prioritize tech-free family time, like dinners or outings, and show genuine interest in their world. Setting shared boundaries around technology and modeling balanced use also helps. When children feel truly understood and valued, they're more open, strengthening the parent-child bond."

Dear Readers,

It's been an enlightening experience addressing these diverse and important topics. We hope our answers provide clarity and support as you navigate your personal and familial journeys.

Remember, whether you're a parent or a youth, you're not alone in facing these challenges. Keep reaching out, stay open to growth, and continue *defying your gravity* together.

Annexure B: Gravity-Defying Voices

Real-Life Inspirations

In this section, we celebrate the Gravity-Defying Voices, the extraordinary individuals who have risen above challenges, redefined the limits of possibility, and left an indelible mark on the world. These are stories of resilience, vision, and unwavering determination, where people like Dr. A.P.J. Abdul Kalam, Ratan Tata, and others have defied the odds, pushing beyond the gravitational pull of doubt, adversity, and limitations. Their journeys remind us that *true* greatness isn't about where you start, but how far you're willing to go, no matter the obstacles.

<u>Dr. A.P.J. Abdul Kalam – From a newspaper seller to India's Missile Man and the President of the country</u>

Dr A.P.J. Abdul Kalam's journey from humble beginnings to becoming the 'Missile Man of India' and the President of the country is a testament to perseverance and dedication. Born on October 15, 1931, in a small coastal town in Tamil Nadu, India, Kalam grew up in a financially constrained household. His father was a boat owner, and his mother was a homemaker. To contribute to his family's income, Kalam started delivering newspapers at a young age. Despite the economic hardships, Kalam was determined to pursue education.

He studied hard, especially in subjects like physics and mathematics, and eventually graduated in aerospace engineering from the Madras Institute of Technology. His entry into the Indian Space Research Organization (ISRO) marked the beginning of his extraordinary career as a scientist. Kalam led many crucial projects, including the development of India's first satellite launch vehicle, SLV-III, which successfully deployed the Rohini satellite in near-earth orbit in 1980.

Kalam's defining moment came when he played a pivotal role in India's missile development programs. He led the Integrated Guided Missile Development Program, which produced missiles like Agni and Prithvi, cementing India's place as a nuclear power. For his immense contribution to science, he became known as the 'Missile Man of India'.

In 2002, Kalam was elected as the President of India. Even as President, he remained connected to the common man and worked to inspire the youth. He authored several books, including Wings of Fire, which narrates his struggles and triumphs.

Inspiration: His life story is one of resilience, self-belief, and the power of dreams. He showed that no matter how challenging life's circumstances, a deep commitment to one's goals can elevate a person to greatness.

Ratan Tata – The Visionary Who Revived an Empire

Ratan Tata, born in 1937 into one of India's most illustrious families, upheld a remarkable legacy as the scion of the Tata Group. Even though he hailed from an iconic business lineage, his journey to becoming one of India's most respected industrialists was marked by doubt and skepticism. When he succeeded J.R.D. Tata, as chairman of the Tata Group in 1991, many within the conglomerate questioned his ability to lead such a vast and diverse empire. At that time, the group spanned industries as varied as steel, automobiles, and telecommunications, and many doubted whether Ratan Tata had the vision or leadership prowess to steer it through changing times. Yet, with quiet determination and a clear vision, Ratan Tata not only met those challenges head-on but transformed the Tata Group into a global powerhouse. He modernized its operations, restructured underperforming companies, and made audacious acquisitions that would define his tenure. One of his most remarkable achievements was the acquisition of Jaguar Land Rover (JLR) by Tata Motors in 2008. Despite a global economic crisis and widespread skepticism about the deal, Tata saw it as an opportunity to elevate Indian industry on the global stage. The acquisition not only revived the luxury car brands but also positioned Tata Motors as a key player in the global automotive market.

Ratan Tata's vision wasn't just limited to large corporations; he was deeply invested in making a difference in the lives of ordinary people. His introduction of the Tata Nano, the world's most affordable car, was a testament to his commitment to social responsibility. While the Nano faced commercial setbacks, its underlying intent—to make personal transportation accessible to the average Indian—reflected Tata's drive to innovate for societal good.

His leadership also extended into philanthropy, with the Tata Trusts contributing a significant portion of the group's profits to causes such as education, healthcare, and rural development. These efforts have positively impacted millions of lives across India, cementing the Tata Group's reputation as a business that cares about people as much as profits.

His leadership is defined not by loud gestures but by quiet resolve, integrity, and a long-term vision. He consistently balanced business success with social responsibility, and his humility in the face of enormous challenges continues to inspire entrepreneurs and leaders across the globe.

Although Ratan Tata is no longer with us, his legacy endures. His life's work—a testament to perseverance, innovation, and a deep commitment to societal betterment—will continue to guide future generations. His vision helped to revive and expand an empire, and his values have left an

Inspiration: Ratan Tata's journey is a powerful reminder that quiet leadership, vision, and perseverance can overcome even the greatest challenges. His humility and dedication continue to inspire entrepreneurs around the world.

Milkha Singh – The Flying Sikh

Milkha Singh, also known as 'The Flying Sikh', is one of India's greatest athletes, whose journey from a war-torn childhood to becoming a legendary sprinter is one of courage, resilience, and indomitable spirit. Born in 1929 in Govindpura, a village that is now part of Pakistan, Milkha's early life was shattered by the Partition of India in 1947. His family was brutally massacred during the riots, and Milkha narrowly escaped death. Traumatized and orphaned, he fled to India as a refugee, enduring a harrowing journey filled with hunger, loss, and despair.

Life in post-Partition India was difficult for Milkha. He lived in refugee camps and took up odd jobs to survive. He eventually joined the Indian Army, and it was here that his talent for running was discovered. His commanding officer noticed his speed during a cross-country race and encouraged him to take up athletics seriously. Milkha seized the opportunity, determined to leave behind the horrors of his past and create a new identity for himself.

Training rigorously, Milkha Singh soon emerged as one of India's best sprinters. He broke the national record in the 400 meters and quickly gained recognition on the international stage. In 1958, he won gold medals in both the 200 meters and 400 meters at the Asian Games, and later that year, he became the first Indian athlete to win a gold medal at the Commonwealth Games in Cardiff, Wales.

Despite his success, Milkha's most significant challenge came at the 1960 Rome Olympics, where he competed in the 400 meters event. Milkha was one of the favorites to win, and the entire nation had its hopes pinned on him. In a race that was fiercely contested, Milkha led for most of the distance but faltered in the final moments. He finished fourth, missing out on an Olympic medal by a fraction of a second. The loss haunted Milkha for the rest of his life, but it did not diminish his incredible achievements.

Milkha Singh continued to represent India at the highest levels of competition, inspiring a generation of athletes. He won gold medals in the 400 meters at the 1962 Asian Games and remained a dominant figure in Indian athletics throughout the 1960s.

Inspiration: His life story was immortalized in the 2013 Bollywood biopic Bhaag Milkha Bhaag, which introduced his journey to a new generation. The film not only depicted his athletic prowess but also the personal struggles he overcame, including the trauma of Partition and the loss of his family.

Mary Kom – Punching Her Way to Glory

Mary Kom's journey from a small village in Manipur to becoming a global icon in boxing is a testament to her relentless spirit, determination, and resilience. Born in 1982 to a family of farmers, Mary Kom grew up in a region with limited resources and opportunities. Her early life was marked by poverty, and she had to juggle household chores and studies, but she was always drawn to sports. Initially, she was interested in athletics, but when she learned about the success of boxer Dingko Singh, who hailed from her home state, Mary was inspired to take up boxing.

Despite her love for the sport, her journey into boxing was far from easy. Her parents disapproved of her choice, fearing that boxing was not suitable for a girl. However, Mary was determined to pursue her passion, and she trained in secret. Her hard work paid off when she started winning local competitions, and soon, her talent caught the attention of coaches at the state level.

Mary Kom's boxing career took off in 2000 when she won her first national championship, followed by several international victories. Despite her success, she faced numerous challenges. In a male-dominated sport, she had to constantly prove herself. Moreover, after getting married and becoming a mother, many doubted her ability to return to the boxing ring. But Mary Kom proved her critics wrong. After giving birth to her first child, she made a stunning comeback and went on to win her fifth World Amateur Boxing Championship in 2010. Her resilience and skill earned her the nickname 'Magnificent Mary'.

In 2012, Mary Kom made history by winning a bronze medal at the London Olympics, becoming the first Indian woman boxer to achieve this feat. She followed this up with more victories, including her sixth

World Championship title in 2018, making her the only woman to achieve such a remarkable record in amateur boxing.

Mary Kom's legacy extends beyond her medals. She has inspired countless young women in India to pursue sports, breaking barriers in a society where women's participation in such fields is often limited. Her life story, filled with personal and professional challenges, highlights her unwavering determination to succeed and the belief that no dream is too big.

Inspiration: Mary Kom's journey from a small village to the global stage is a powerful example of how hard work, passion, and resilience can overcome any obstacle.

Sudha Chandran – Dancing Through Adversity

Sudha Chandran was a rising star in the world of classical Indian dance when her life took a tragic turn. In 1981, at the age of 16, Sudha was involved in a road accident that resulted in her right leg being amputated due to medical complications. For many, this would have been the end of a promising dancing career, but not for Sudha Chandran.

Sudha's spirit was unyielding, and her passion for dance never faltered. After months of rehabilitation, she was fitted with a prosthetic leg known as the Jaipur foot. Despite the pain and challenges of dancing with an artificial limb, Sudha was determined to return to the stage. It wasn't an easy journey, she faced excruciating pain, doubts from others, and her own frustrations. However, her perseverance pushed her forward.

In a few years, Sudha not only regained her ability to dance but performed across India and the world, receiving standing ovations. She made her comeback with a stage performance in Mumbai that left the audience in awe. Sudha's incredible willpower and determination helped her overcome the physical and mental challenges she faced. She also ventured into acting and became a well-known television and film actress.

Inspiration: Sudha Chandran's story is not just about reclaiming her passion; it's about resilience and defying the odds. She showed the world that physical limitations cannot stop a person who has the will to fight back. Today, she continues to inspire countless people with her story of courage, resilience, and triumph over adversity.

<u>Arunima Sinha – From Train Tragedy to Scaling Everest</u>

Arunima Sinha was a national-level volleyball player with dreams of representing India when tragedy struck in 2011. While traveling by train, she resisted a gang of thieves who attempted to steal her bag. In the struggle, Arunima was thrown out of the moving train. She fell onto the tracks, and another train ran over her leg, leading to its amputation.

For many, this would have been the end of their athletic aspirations, but not for Arunima. As she lay in the hospital, battling despair, she made an extraordinary decision: she would climb Mount Everest. People around her doubted her ability to even walk properly, let alone scale the world's highest peak. But Arunima's determination was unshakable. After receiving a prosthetic leg, she began her intensive training for mountaineering.

Arunima trained rigorously, enduring both physical and mental challenges. In 2013, just two years after her accident, she made history by becoming the first female amputee to climb Mount Everest. The journey was grueling, with extreme weather conditions and a physically taxing climb, but Arunima's willpower carried her through.

Her story does not stop with Everest. Arunima went on to scale other major peaks across the world, becoming a symbol of resilience and determination. She has since become a motivational speaker, inspiring millions with her incredible story of overcoming extreme adversity.

Inspiration: Arunima's journey is a powerful reminder that even in the face of the most unimaginable challenges, the human spirit can rise to extraordinary heights.

Dhirubhai Ambani – From Petrol Pump Attendant to Industrial Tycoon

Dhirubhai Ambani's story is a classic tale of rags to riches, filled with lessons of perseverance, business acumen, and determination. Born in a small village in Gujarat in 1932, Dhirubhai came from a modest background. His father was a schoolteacher, and the family struggled to make ends meet. At the age of 16, Dhirubhai moved to Yemen to work as a petrol pump attendant and a clerk in a trading company.

Despite the odds, Dhirubhai had big dreams of becoming an entrepreneur. He returned to India in the 1950s and began his journey by trading in spices and fabrics. In 1966, with limited capital, he founded Reliance Industries, initially focusing on the textile industry. Dhirubhai's ability to foresee market trends, coupled with his relentless work ethic, helped him navigate India's often challenging business environment.

Through sheer persistence and innovative business strategies, Dhirubhai expanded Reliance into a vast empire that diversified into petrochemicals, telecommunications, and energy. By the time of his death in 2002, Reliance had become one of India's largest and most successful conglomerates, and Dhirubhai Ambani had become a legend in Indian business history.

Inspiration: His story is an example of how vision, hard work, and the ability to adapt to changing circumstances can turn an ordinary man into one of the most successful businessmen in the world. Dhirubhai's life continues to inspire aspiring entrepreneurs to dream big and persist despite challenges.

<u>J.K. Rowling – From Poverty to Bestselling Author</u>

J.K. Rowling's journey to becoming one of the most famous and successful authors in the world is a tale of perseverance, rejection, and, finally, triumph. Born in England, Rowling always had a passion for storytelling. However, her path to success was anything but easy. In the early 1990s, Rowling faced significant hardships, she was a single mother living on welfare, struggling to make ends meet after the death of her mother and the end of her marriage.

During these difficult years, Rowling began writing the first Harry Potter book, often working in cafes with her infant daughter by her side. She completed the manuscript for Harry Potter and the Philosopher's Stone but faced rejection after rejection from publishers. In fact, the manuscript was rejected by 12 different publishers before Bloomsbury finally agreed to publish it in 1997.

The rest, as they say, is history. The Harry Potter series became a global phenomenon, selling over 500 million copies worldwide and making J.K. Rowling one of the wealthiest women in the world. But Rowling's journey is more than a success story; it's about defying self-doubt, societal pressure, and personal struggles to follow one's passion. She often speaks about the importance of failure and how hitting rock bottom became the foundation on which she rebuilt her life.

Inspiration: Rowling's story is an inspiring example of how persistence, belief in oneself, and the power of imagination can transform life's most difficult moments into extraordinary success.

<u>Oprah Winfrey – Rising Above a Troubled Childhood</u>

Oprah Winfrey is now synonymous with success, philanthropy, and resilience, but her journey to becoming one of the most influential women in the world was filled with hardship. Born in rural Mississippi to a teenage single mother in 1954, Oprah's early life was marked by poverty, neglect, and abuse. She moved between her grandmother, mother, and father, facing sexual abuse from family members as a young girl, and later became pregnant at the age of 14. Her son, born prematurely, died in infancy.

Despite the traumatic events of her childhood, Oprah found solace in education. She excelled at school, became an honors student, and won a scholarship to Tennessee State University. At 19, she began her career in media as a news anchor, but it wasn't long before her unique style of emotional engagement led her to host a talk show in Chicago.

In 1986, The Oprah Winfrey Show debuted nationally, quickly becoming the highest-rated talk show in television history. Oprah's empathetic interviewing style and willingness to discuss taboo subjects resonated with millions. Beyond her success in television, Oprah became a media mogul, launching her own production company, a magazine, and even a television network, OWN.

Oprah's story is not only one of overcoming personal hardship but also one of leveraging her success to uplift others. She has donated millions to educational causes, opened a leadership academy for girls in South Africa, and continues to use her platform to inspire and bring about change.

Inspiration: Oprah Winfrey's journey embodies resilience, proving that no matter the challenges, one can rise to become a force for good.

<u>Stephen Hawking – Defying ALS to Unlock the Secrets of the Universe</u>

Stephen Hawking's story is one of triumph over physical adversity. Born in Oxford, England, in 1942, Hawking showed an early aptitude for mathematics and physics, eventually earning a spot at the University of Cambridge to study cosmology. At the age of 21, while still a student, Hawking was diagnosed with amyotrophic lateral sclerosis (ALS), a neurodegenerative disease that gradually paralyzed him. Doctors gave him only two years to live.

Despite this grim diagnosis, Hawking defied expectations and continued his studies. He went on to make groundbreaking contributions to theoretical physics, particularly in the fields of black holes and cosmology. His theory that black holes emit radiation, now known as Hawking radiation, revolutionized the way scientists understand the universe.

Although the disease confined him to a wheelchair and eventually took away his ability to speak, Hawking never let his physical limitations define him. He communicated through a speech-generating device and continued to publish scientific papers, give lectures, and write books, including the international bestseller A Brief History of Time, which brought complex scientific ideas to a global audience.

Hawking's resilience and intellectual achievements made him one of the most famous and respected scientists of his time.

Inspiration: His life is an extraordinary example of how the mind can overcome even the most severe physical disabilities. Hawking once said, "However difficult life may seem, there is always something you can do and succeed at." His legacy continues to inspire countless individuals to push the boundaries of what is possible.

<u>Elon Musk – Pushing the Boundaries of Technology</u>

Elon Musk, the founder of SpaceX and Tesla, is widely regarded as one of the most innovative and ambitious entrepreneurs of the modern era. However, his path to success has been anything but easy. Born in South Africa in 1971, Musk faced a troubled childhood marked by bullying and family strife. He was passionate about technology from a young age and taught himself programming at just 12 years old.

Musk left South Africa to attend college in the United States, where he pursued degrees in physics and economics. After co-founding several startups, including Zip2 and PayPal, Musk set his sights on the future of humanity, developing sustainable energy solutions and space exploration. In 2002, he founded SpaceX to reduce space transportation costs and eventually enable human colonization of Mars. However, the company faced numerous failures and near bankruptcy. Musk's relentless drive kept the company afloat, and in 2008, SpaceX became the first privately funded company to send a spacecraft to the International Space Station.

Simultaneously, Musk revolutionized the automobile industry with Tesla Motors, a company he co-founded that aimed to make electric cars mainstream. Like SpaceX, Tesla faced financial struggles and production delays, but Musk's vision paid off. Today, Tesla is a leader in the electric vehicle market and renewable energy solutions.

Inspiration: Musk's story is one of unyielding ambition, risk-taking, and a relentless pursuit of technological innovation. His willingness to push boundaries and challenge established industries has made him a figure of inspiration for many aspiring entrepreneurs and innovators worldwide. Despite the countless setbacks, Musk continues to defy the odds, proving that with vision, resilience, and risk-taking, one can reshape the future.

Dear Readers,

Reflection: "Who is someone you admire for their perseverance? What qualities do they embody that you want to cultivate in yourself?"

Action Step: Choose one role model and research their story. Write down three qualities they exhibit that resonate with you. How can you start incorporating those qualities into your daily life?

____

1. ___________________________________

2. ___________________________________

3. ___________________________________

Annexure C: Evolving Brains – I

Parenting Wisdom: Quotes to Guide and Support

1. *"To be in your children's memories tomorrow, you have to be in their lives today." – Barbara Johnson*

   Make quality time with your children a priority.

2. *"Children are not a distraction from more important work. They are the most important work." – C.S. Lewis*

   Parenting is a crucial role that shapes future generations.

3. *"The greatest legacy we can leave our children is happy memories." – OG Mandino*

   Create joyful moments that your children will cherish forever.

4. *"Your children will become who you are; so be who you want them to be." – David Bly*

   Lead by example; your actions speak louder than words.

5. *"A child's first teacher is its mother." – Peng Liyuan*

   Parental influence is foundational for a child's growth and development.

6. *"There is no such thing as a perfect parent. So just be a real one." – Sue Atkins*

   Embrace authenticity in parenting and be yourself.

7. *"In parenting, there are no mistakes, only lessons." – Anonymous*

   Every experience is an opportunity to learn and grow together.

8. *"The way we talk to our children becomes their inner voice." – Peggy O'Mara*

   Use encouraging language that helps build their self-esteem.

9. *"It takes a village to raise a child." – African Proverb*

   Community support is essential in nurturing and guiding children.

10. *"There is no greater force for change than a parent's love." – Anonymous*

Annexure D: Evolving Brains – II

Empowering Youth: Inspirational Quotes for Your Journey Ahead

1. *"The future belongs to those who believe in the beauty of their dreams." – Eleanor Roosevelt*

   Dreams are powerful; believe in them and pursue them.

2. *"What lies behind us and what lies before us are tiny matters compared to what lies within us." – Ralph Waldo Emerson*

   Your inner strength and determination shape your future.

3. *"You miss 100% of the shots you don't take." – Wayne Gretzky*

   Take risks and seize opportunities; don't let fear hold you back.

4. *"Success is not the key to happiness. Happiness is the key to success. If you love what you are doing, you will be successful." – Albert Schweitzer*

   Find joy in your pursuits; that's where true success lies.

5. *"Your life is your story, and the adventure ahead of you is the journey to fulfill your own purpose and potential." – Kerry Washington*

   Own your narrative and pursue your passions.

6. *"Do not wait to strike till the iron is hot, but make it hot by striking." – William Butler Yeats*

   Take initiative and create your own opportunities.

7. *"You are never too young to start making a difference." – Anonymous*

   Your actions, no matter how small, can have a significant impact.

8. *"Success is not how high you have climbed, but how you make a positive difference to the world." – Roy T. Bennett*

   Focus on contributing to the greater good in your journey.

9. *"Don't watch the clock; do what it does. Keep going." – Sam Levenson*

   Persevere and keep moving forward, regardless of challenges.

10. *"Your time is limited, so don't waste it living someone else's life." – Steve Jobs*

    Stay true to yourself and follow your unique path.

Annexure E: Evolving Brains – III

Seeds of Wisdom: Encouraging Quotes for Young Learners

1. *"You are braver than you believe, stronger than you seem, and smarter than you think." – A.A. Milne*

   Believe in your own abilities and never underestimate your potential.

2. *"Mistakes are proof that you are trying." – Jennifer Lim*

   Don't be afraid to make mistakes; they are part of learning and growing.

3. *"You have brains in your head. You have feet in your shoes. You can steer yourself any direction you choose." – Dr. Seuss*

   You have the power to make choices and create your own path in life.

4. *"It's not what happens to you, but how you react to it that matters." – Epictetus*

   Your reactions and attitude shape your experiences more than the events themselves.

5. *"The only limit to our realization of tomorrow will be our doubts of today." – Franklin D. Roosevelt*

   Believe in your dreams, and don't let doubts hold you back.

6. *"You are never too old to set another goal or to dream a new dream." – C.S. Lewis*

   It's never too late to pursue new interests or aspirations.

7. *"Believe you can, and you're halfway there." – Theodore Roosevelt*

    Confidence is a key step toward achieving your goals.

8. *"If you can dream it, you can do it." – Walt Disney*

    Your dreams are achievable if you work hard to make them a reality.

9. *"The more that you read, the more things you will know. The more that you learn, the more places you'll go." – Dr. Seuss*

    Education opens doors to endless opportunities.

10. *"It's not about how hard you hit. It's about how hard you can get hit and keep moving forward." – Rocky Balboa*

    Resilience is essential; keep pushing through challenges.

Annexure F: Understanding NLP

A Simple Guide

We're excited to chat with you about something that might sound a bit complex at first but trust us; it's super interesting: ***Neuro-Linguistic Programming, or NLP for short!***

Think of NLP as a toolbox filled with handy tools that help you understand how your brain works, how you communicate with yourself and others, and how you can change the way you think to lead a happier, more fulfilling life.

So, let's break it down!

At its core, NLP is all about the connection between our thoughts (that's the 'Neuro' part), our language (the 'Linguistic' bit), and our behaviors (the 'Programming' piece). It's kind of like having a guidebook for your mind! So, what do each of those parts mean?

- Well, *'Neuro'* refers to your brain and nervous system. It's all about understanding how your thoughts affect your feelings and actions.

- *'Linguistic'* is about language, how you communicate with yourself and others. The words you choose can really shape your reality, you know?

- And then there's *'Programming'*. Just like a computer program runs based on a set of instructions, NLP helps you change your mental 'programming' to create more positive outcomes in your life.

So, you might be wondering, "Why did we decide to include NLP in Defy Your Gravity?"

Well, if you really wondered about that, trust us, it's a great question! There are a few reasons:

- ***First off, it's all about empowerment.*** NLP gives you the tools to take control of your thoughts and emotions. When Aadi, our main character, learns about NLP techniques, he realizes he can change his perspective on challenges and failures. That empowerment is such a key theme in the book. We want you to embrace your own power too!

- And let's not forget about **better communication**. Aadi struggles with how to talk to his family and himself. Using NLP, he learns to express his feelings more clearly and listen effectively. That ***boosts his confidence big time!***

- Plus, we all face setbacks in life, right? ***With NLP, we can reframe those failures into opportunities for growth.*** Aadi's journey shows that looking at failures differently can lead to personal transformation.

- And we wanted to make sure Defy Your Gravity is practical! NLP gives you real-life tools you can use to improve your situation. Whether it's setting achievable goals or using positive language, there are actionable steps for you to follow. The techniques Aadi uses can be applied in your life, turning reading into an interactive experience!

So, remember that NLP isn't just fancy terminology; it's a way to unlock your potential and change your life for the better.

Summarized NLP Techniques

Reframing: The process of changing the way we perceive a situation to alter its meaning. For instance, viewing a setback as a learning opportunity instead of a failure.

Anchoring: A technique where a specific stimulus (like a touch or a word) is associated with a particular emotional state, allowing you to recreate that feeling when needed. For example, remembering a moment of confidence before a public speaking engagement.

Pacing: Matching the rhythm and tone of another person's communication style to create rapport and make them feel more at ease.

Mirroring: Subtly mimicking the body language or speech patterns of someone you are communicating with to build a connection and to build trust.

Meta-Model Questions: A set of specific questions designed to clarify vague or ambiguous statements. For example, asking, "What specifically do you mean by that?" helps to get to the heart of a conversation.

Step-by-Step Instructions

For each technique, here's a brief, actionable guide:

Reframing: Identify a negative belief, write it down, and rephrase it positively.

Anchoring: Choose a physical gesture (like pressing your thumb and forefinger together) and associate it with a positive experience. Practice it until the gesture triggers that feeling.

Pacing: During a conversation, observe the other person's tone and pace and adjust your own to match.

Mirroring: Watch for the other person's body language; gently mimic their posture or gestures to establish rapport.

Meta-Model Questions: Used in conversations to enhance clarity, for example, "Can you tell me more about that?"

The Power of Reframing

Rise Above Your Challenges and Embrace Your Potential

We all face tough times, don't we? There are moments when life throws us a curveball, and it's easy to get caught up in negative thoughts. But here's the thing: what if you could choose how to see those challenges? That's where reframing comes in!

Think of reframing like putting on a new pair of glasses. With your old glasses, a situation might seem bleak or overwhelming. But once you change the lens, the picture changes! Suddenly, what seemed like a setback is now a setup for growth.

Here's a handy chart to help you reframe some common challenges you might face. As you go through these scenarios, try applying them to your own life. Whenever you're feeling down or stuck, take a moment to pause and see if you can shift your perspective.

Negative Scenarios vs Positive Reframes

S. NO	NEGATIVE SCENARIO	NEGATIVE THOUGHT	REFRAMED POSITIVE THOUGHT
1.	Failing an exam	"I'm a failure. I'll never be good at this subject."	"This was a tough exam, but now I know what I need to work on for next time."
2.	Rejected from a Job Interview	"I'm not good enough. No one will hire me."	"This wasn't the right fit for me, but it's great practice for the next one."

S. NO	NEGATIVE SCENARIO	NEGATIVE THOUGHT	REFRAMED POSITIVE THOUGHT
3.	Conflict with a Friend	"I'm not good enough. No one will hire me."	"This wasn't the right fit for me, but it's great practice for the next one."
4.	Being Criticized by a Teacher or Parent	"They think I'm useless and will never succeed."	"They care enough to want me to improve. I'll focus on what I can learn from this."
5.	Feeling Left Out of a Social Event	"Nobody wants me around. I'm not important to them."	"Maybe they didn't realize I wanted to join. Next time, I'll speak up!"
6.	Not Getting into Your Dream College	"I worked so hard, and it was all for nothing."	"One path didn't work out, but there are many other opportunities to explore."
7.	Losing a Sports Match or Competition	"I let my team down. I'm not cut out for this."	"Today wasn't our day, but I'm proud of the effort I put in. Let's aim to improve!"
8.	Not Meeting Family Expectations	"I'm always disappointing them. I'll never be enough."	"Their expectations are high, but I'm on my own path, growing at my own pace."
9.	Struggling with Body Image	"I hate how I look. I'm not attractive."	"I have many qualities beyond appearance, and I'm learning to appreciate myself."
10.	Being Overwhelmed by Social Media Comparisons	"Everyone else is doing so much better than me."	"Social media only shows highlights. I'm focused on my own journey and progress."

<u>Let's Break It Down to Exactly How to Reframe Your Own Thoughts</u>

1.   *Identify the Negative Thought*

First, become aware of the negative thoughts you're having. Write it down if that helps! For example: *"I'm terrible at public speaking."*

2.   *Challenge the Thought*

Ask yourself: Is this really true? What evidence do I have to support this? What evidence contradicts it? Often, we find that our negative thoughts are exaggerated.

3.   *Find a Positive Twist*

*Look for a way to flip the situation. Instead of saying, "I'm terrible at public speaking," try saying, **"I'm just starting out, but every time I speak, I'm getting better and more confident."***

4.   *Anchor It with a Positive Action*

After reframing, take a small positive action that reinforces the new thought. If you reframed your public speaking fear, take one small step: ***practice in front of a mirror or record yourself speaking.***

Aadi's Reframing Practice
Let's see how Aadi applied this in his own life!

Scenario:
After being rejected from a job interview, Aadi initially thought, "I'm never going to find a job. I'm not good enough."

Challenge:
His mother asked, "Is that really true, Aadi? What about the skills you've gained and the positive feedback you received during the interview?"

Reframe:
Aadi realized, "The interview didn't go as I'd hoped, but it taught me what to focus on next time."

Positive Action:
Aadi decided to join a mock interview group to get more comfortable with the process.

By reframing the situation, Aadi turned rejection into motivation for improvement!

Reflection for You

Think about a time when you felt defeated or frustrated. What was your initial negative thought? Write it down:

Negative Thought: ____

Now, take a moment to reframe it. What is a more positive, empowering way to see this situation?

Reframed Thought: ____

What's one small action you can take to support this new thought?

Action: ____

Key Takeaway

Reframing isn't about ignoring the challenges you face. It's about choosing to see them from a different angle, one that empowers you rather than holds you back. With practice, you can train your mind to look for the opportunity within every obstacle.

So, the next time life throws you a curveball, grab that toolbox called Reframing and turn that negative into a stepping stone toward growth and success!

Annexure G

Reflection Journal Pages

These blank pages are your personal space for journaling. Use them to capture your thoughts, reflections, and experiences as you progress. Write freely and reflect on your journey, your growth starts here!

Annexure G

Reflection Journal Pages

Annexure G

Reflection Journal Pages

Annexure H

The Power of Gratitude

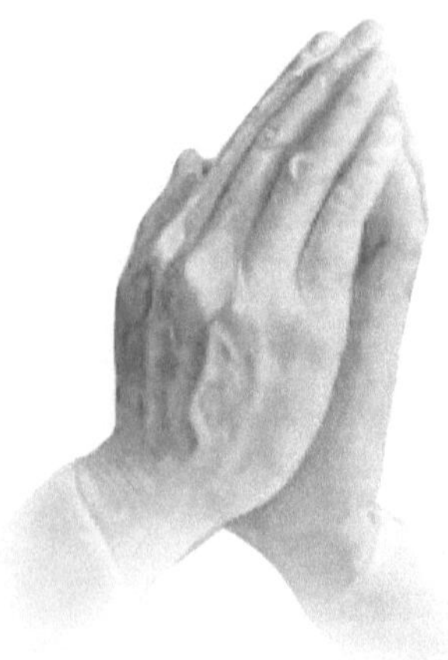

*A*s our journey comes to an end, both of us want to share with you something we believe in immensely and something that can truly change your life, too: **gratitude.**

We touched on the importance of gratitude in Aadi's story, but honestly, since it's something we believe in and practice so much, we felt it deserves its own space in the book.

We also know you've probably heard a lot about gratitude already, but stick with us for a minute. **Gratitude is more than just saying 'thank you'** when someone holds the door open for you. It's about shifting your focus. Instead of seeing what's missing in your life, it helps you see all the wonderful things that are already there.

We've all been through tough times, haven't we? And trust us, it's not always easy to find the silver lining. But here's the magic: when you make gratitude a daily habit, it actually changes how you see the world. And, spoiler alert, it makes everything feel a little brighter!

Why Gratitude is a Game-Changer

Drishti: *Let's talk about why gratitude is such a big deal. It literally rewires your brain. When you focus on what you're grateful for, it's like your brain says, "Oh, so this is what matters!" It starts looking for the good stuff more often. And that makes life feel more positive, even when things are hard.*

Neha: *Exactly! It also helps with relationships. The more you show appreciation to the people around you, the closer and more connected you feel to them. Trust us on this, it works wonders.*

And the best part? It builds resilience. Gratitude doesn't mean ignoring your problems, but it does give you the strength to see challenges as opportunities for growth. It's like an emotional muscle you can build over time!

How You Can Practice Gratitude

How do you actually do this whole gratitude thing? Well, it's super simple! Here are some ways you can start practicing gratitude today:

1. **Gratitude Journal**

   Take just a few minutes at the end of each day to jot down three things you're grateful for. They can be as small as a smile from a stranger or as big as nailing a big project at work.

2. **Gratitude in the Moment**

   When something goes right, even something small, pause and take a second to appreciate it. It could be a sunny day, a good meal, or an unexpected message from a friend.

3. Gratitude for Others

Make it a habit to tell people you appreciate them. Maybe it's a text to your best friend or a thank you note to someone who helped you out recently. You'd be amazed at how much these small gestures can mean.

4. Gratitude in Hard Times

OK, this one's a bit tricky, but it's the most powerful. When something doesn't go as planned, try to find one small thing to be grateful for. Maybe it's the lesson you learned or the strength you built. You won't believe how this mindset shift can turn things around!

Aadi's Gratitude Journey

Aadi had his share of ups and downs. But one thing that really helped him stay grounded was practicing gratitude. Even on his toughest days, he learned to find something or anything he could appreciate. Maybe it was his mother's support, or maybe it was just getting through a rough day.

And it wasn't just about the good stuff. Aadi learned to appreciate the hard times, too, because those were the moments that pushed him to grow.

Your Turn: Try It Out!

Now it's your turn! Let's put this into practice. We've left space here for you to jot down three things you're grateful for today. It can be anything, big or small. Don't overthink it, just write down what comes to mind.

What are three things you're grateful for today?

1. ____

2. ____

3. ____

Who is someone you can thank today for making your life better?

1. ____

2. ____

3. ____

What's one challenge you've faced recently that you can reframe as a chance to grow?

1. ____

2. ____

3. ____

The more you practice gratitude, the easier it gets to see the good in every situation. And guess what? It's a tool you can use anytime, anywhere.

Final Thoughts from Us

Drishti: *Gratitude is like a secret superpower. It helps you rise above the noise, the stress, and the chaos of life. And once you get into the habit, it becomes second nature.*

Neha: *We hope this little section on gratitude inspires you to make it a part of your daily routine. No matter where you are in your journey, there's always something to be thankful for, even if it's just the chance to start again.*

So, what are you grateful for today?

Go ahead, embrace it and let gratitude lift you up to new heights!

Thank you for being part of this transformative journey of

Defying Your Gravity!